Probate Records of South Carolina

Volume I: Index to Inventories 1746-1785

Compiled by:
Brent Holcomb

Southern Historical Press, Inc.
Greenville, South Carolina

Copyrigth 1977 by:
Southern Historical Press, Inc.

All rights reserved. No part of this publication may be
reproduced, stored in a retrieval system or transmitted
in any form or by any means without the
prior permission of the publisher.

SOUTHERN HISTORICAL PRESS, INC.
PO BOX 1267
Greenville, SC   29601

ISBN #0-89308-052-7

Printed in the United States of America

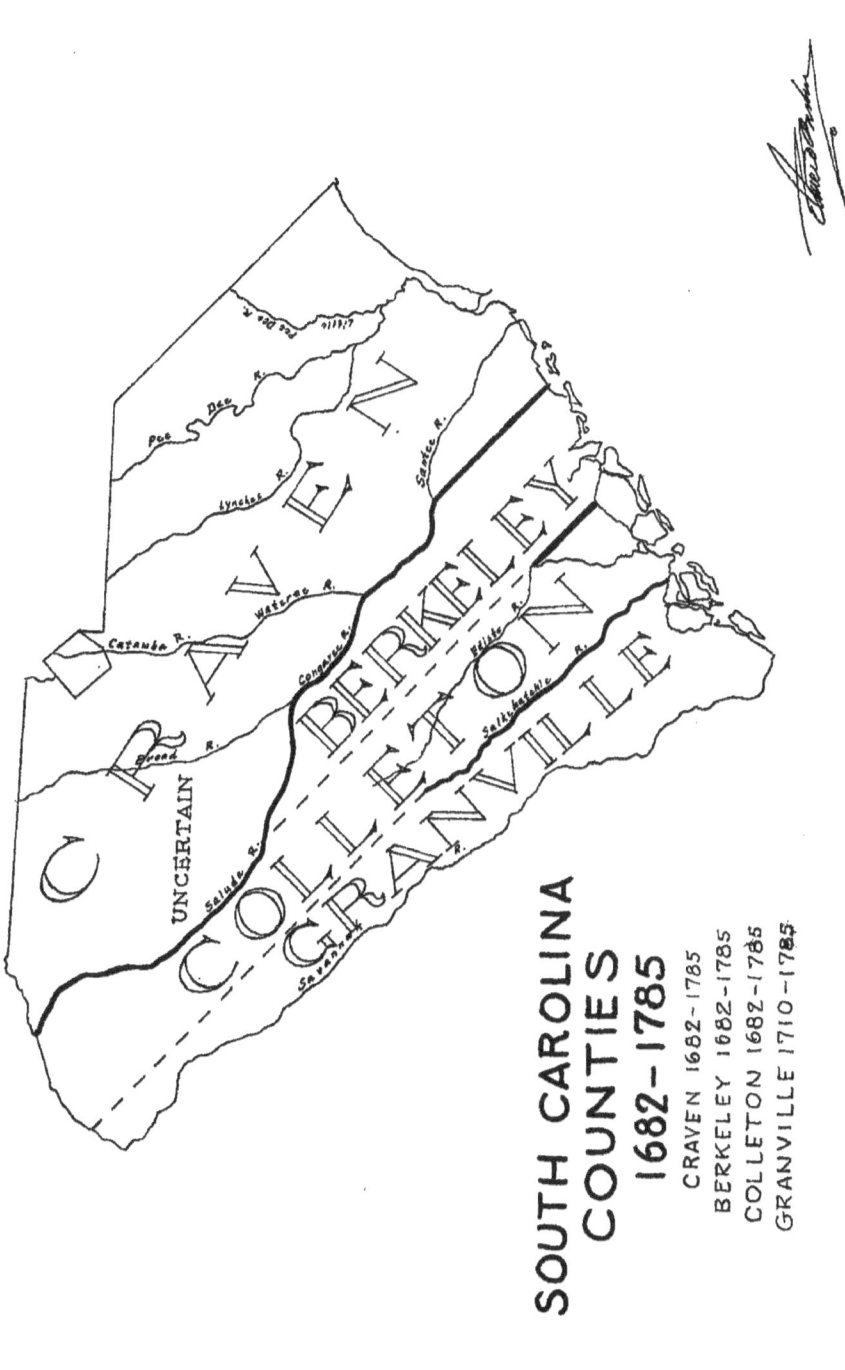

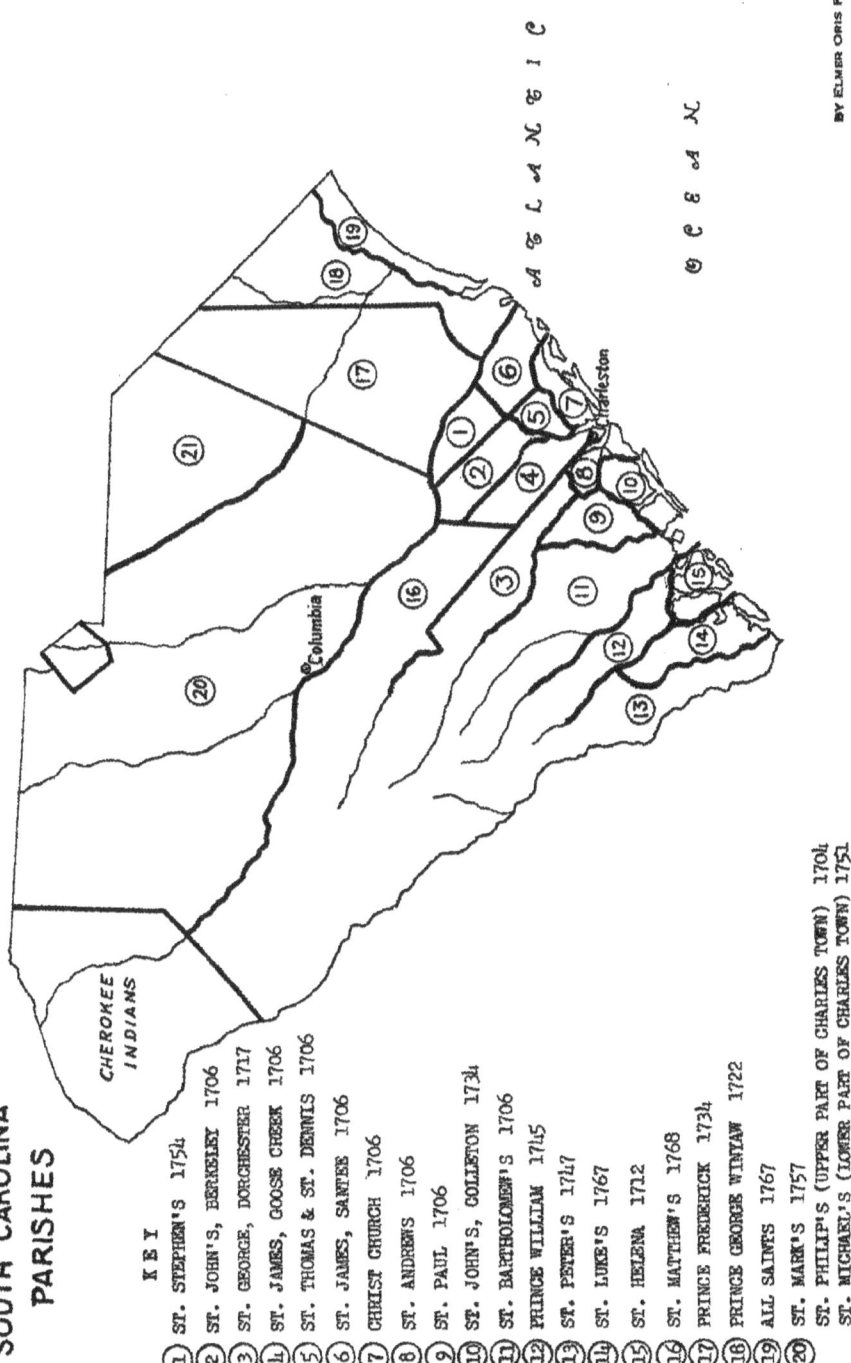

INTRODUCTION

The Inventories of South Carolina are a set of records used more often by historical researchers rather than genealogists. This is unfortunate, as inventories often contain little nuggets of information for the family researcher. First of all, these records are generally misunderstood. As one would expect, they contain lists of personal property for persons deceased intestate. These are the largest part of the intestate records for the Colonial and Revolutionary periods. In addition, these volumes contain inventories for testate persons, sales of estates (often showing purchasers), and divisions of estates. Almost always the names of the appraisers are given, and often the name(s) of the administrator(s) or executor(s). Many of these are not dated, but an approximate date can sometimes be determined by information within the inventory or by the guide to the volumes on the following page. Locations are infrequently given, and then in various and sundry manners--District, Parish, County, River, Township, Town, etc.

This index will make these volumes a more usable tool. There are actually twenty volumes of such inventories. This index covers only the last fiftenn of these (1746-1785), because the first five volumes are incorporated into an index of miscellaneous records available at the South Carolina Archives and the Probate Judge's Office in Charleston. The inventory volumes are in a veried state of preservation. Some are in excellent conditions, others have gaping holes in many of the pages. For this reason, some names cannot be read in the original. However, most of the obliterated names were determined by use of the original indices found in a few of the volumes, by comparison with the WPA copies and by use of L. D. S. microfilm. It may seem odd to have used the last two methods, but these volumes were in better condition when these copies and film were made. When any name has been determined in such a way, it has been put in brackets ([ ]). For the reasons above stated, the originals, WPA copies and LDS microfilm should be used as a set. In each case copies can be obtained from the S. C. Archives for their photostat charges ($1.35 per page plus $1.00 handling per volume). Because the cost of a long inventory could be prohibitive, it is strongly urged that one view the original or have a researcher do so before ordering copies.

Upon first look, the price of this volume may seem large. Keep in mind that many hours were spent preparing this index. I have turned every page of these fifteen volumes, and I have spent time viewing the microfilm copies and WPA copies when necessary.

My thank to Dr. Charles H. Lesser for his helpful suggestions, and to the search room staff at the South Carolina Archives for pulling these volumes for me numerous times.

Brent H. Holcomb, G. R. S.
February 1, 1977

Guide to Inventory Volumes

Archives Control Number	Volume	Years
6	MM	1746-1748
7	B	1748-1751
8	R(1)	1751-1753
9	R(2)	1753-1756
10	S	1756-1758
11	T	1758-1761
12	V	1761-1763
13	*W	1763-1767
14	X	1768-1769
15	Y	1769-1771
16	Z	1771-1774
17	&	1772-1776
18	AA	1774-1785
19	BB	1776-1784
20	CC	1776-1778

*This volume actually bears no letter, only the years, but has been lettered "W" for convenience. The volumes from 1736-1746 (control numbers 1-5) are not included in this index, since those volumes are incorporated into an index of Miscellaneous records available at the South Carolina Archives.

Name	Date	Location	Vol. & pages	
Name obliterated			V	213-214
Name obliterated			V	214-215
No name	18 Aug 1753		R(2)	46-47
No name	21 Apr 1756		R(2)	435-436
No name	29 Mar 1756		R(2)	454
No name	20 Aug 1756		R(2)	522
No name			V	498-499
No name	8 Feb 1771		Y	396
Ackerman, Albert	15 Apr 1767	Granville Co.	W	414-415
Ackerman, George	20 Jan 1774	Prince Wm Parish	Z	455-456
Ackles, Mrs. Margaret	22 Apr 1755	Charles Town	R(2)	324
Adams, George Horatio	25 Aug 1777		AA	258-259
Adams, Isaac	6 May 1765	Edisto Island	W	258-259
Adams, John	29 Jan 1781		BB	118-120
Adams, Joseph	27 Feb 1775		AA	90-93
Adams, Nathaniel	1 May 1763	St. Helina	V	385-386
Adams, Nathaniel	21 Mar 1769	Hilton Head	X	439-440
Adams, William	22 Apr 1756		R(2)	480-483
Adamson, James	22 Jan 1761		T	483
Addison, Allen	7 Dec 1774	Ninety Six District	AA	40-41
Affleck, Thomas	21 Aug 1758		T	53-54
Ainger, Jno			R(1)	394-395
Ainger, John			S	381-382
Ainslee, John	21 Apr 1774	Windser Hill	&	341-344
Ainslee, John	14 May 1774	St. Mathews Parish, Santee	&	344-345
Air, Mrs. Ann	18 May 1764		W	91-95
Air, Dr. James	19 Dec 1777		CC	398-400
Air, William	4 Sept 1754		R(2)	239-242
Aish, Marmaduke	8 July 1750	Charles Town	B	337-338
Aish, Marmaduke	28 Sep		R(1)	455-456
Aitken, William			CC	281
Akehead, William	15 May 1771		Z	47-48
Akehead, William	15 May 1771		Z	53
Akin, Elizabeth spinster	15 Nov 1763	St. Philips Parish, Charles Town	V	522-524
Akin, James	8 Dec 1758		T	118-123
Akin, James	21 May 1781	Charlestown	BB	174-177
Akin, Thos	29 Sep 1781		BB	214
Akins, James	5 May 1759		T	192-195
Akins, Mrs. Margaret	17 Dec 1757		S	243-252
Aldridge, Michael	26 Sep 1763		W	6
Aldridge, William	11 Feb 1778		CC	404-405
Alen, William	18 Apr 1750		B	280-283
Alexander, David	27 Oct 1746		MM	90-91
Alexander, David			X	353
Alexander, David	28 Feb 1754		R(2)	101
Alexander, Peter	24 Mar 1774	St. Pauls Parish	Z	528-530
Alison, Rev. Hector	20 Jan 1768		X	260-262
Allen, Ambrose	4 Jan 1777		BB	19
Allen, James			W	29-30
Allen, James			W	37-38
Allen, James	27 Jul 1767	St. Mark's Parish	X	166
Allen, John	5 Feb 1748/9	Charles Town	B	31-34
Allen, Joseph	26 May 1773		&	252
Allen, Mary	9 Jul 1750		B	303-304
Allen, Sarah widow	14 Mar 1748/9	Chas. Town	B	79-80
Allison, George	12 May 1769	St. Lukes Parish	X	458-459
Allison, Revd. John			X	147-148
Allison, Joseph			B	408
Allison, Robert	16 Jul 1770		Y	317
Allison, Thomas			V	347
Allston, John			B	310-314
Allston, John Jr.			R(1)	306-308
Allston, Josias	3 & 4 Mar 1777	Little River, Prince George Parish	CC	358-364
Allston, Sarah	2 May 1764		W	60
Allston, William	14 Jun 1744		MM	14-15

Name	Date	Location	Vol. & pages	
Alston, Peter	4 Jul 1749		B	130
Amey free Negroe	23 Oct 1770	Charles Town	Y	349
Amey, William	15 Feb 1750/1		B	378
Amory, Sarah	29 Sep 1770		Y	351-352
Amos, Jno.	3 Mar 1749/50	St. George's Parish	R(2)	32
Amoss, James	21 Jul 1755	Charlestown	AA	119-120
Ancrum, George Junr			BB	152-153
Anderson, Abraham			W	247-248
Anderson, Abraham	25 Sep 1765		W	248
Anderson, Abraham Senr.	17 Nov 1767		W	365
Anderson, Alexander	30 Sept 1765		W	276-277
Anderson, David	19 Apr 1775		AA	98
Anderson, Revd. George	5 Dec 1752	Pon Pon	R(1)	510-511
Anderson, Henry	9 Jul 1768		X	393
Anderson, Hugh	2 Mar 1748/9		B	76-77
Anderson, Hugh	15 & 17 June 1763		V	465-467
Anderson, James	14 Feb 1771		Y	422
Anderson, John	14 Jun 1762		V	239-240
Anderson, John			X	197
Anderson, John	14 Aug 1769		Y	113
Anderson, John	13 Feb 1773	Ninety Six	&	209
Anderson, Joseph	7 Jan 1765	St. James Santee	W	194-195
Anderson, Joshua	4 Jul 1769		Y	174-177
Anderson, Thomas	12 Jul 1777		BB	71
Anderson, William	22 Nov 1746		MM	51-52
Anderson, William	12 Mar 1760		T	284-285
Anderson, William	27 Oct 1761	St. Johns [Parish]	V	75-77
Andrea, George	12 Apr 1753	Black River	R(2)	9
Andrews, Joseph Jr.	2 Aug 1759		B	148
Anond, Robt.			Y	9-10
Arbuthnot, Francis	Sep 1776		AA	153-154
Archer, James	5 Jan 1748/9		B	26
Arden, Joseph	2 May 1762	St. George Parish	V	242
Armstrong, Charles	9 Oct 1749	St. Pauls Parish, Collenton County	B	197-198
Armstrong, James	7 Dec 1751	Williamsburgh	R(1)	152
Armstrong, Janet	20 Jun 1754	Williamsburgh	R(2)	242-243
Armstrong, John			Z	233
Arnest, Anthony	5 May 1774		&	426-427
Arnett, John		Williamsburgh	CC	340
Arnold, Thomas	11 Dec 1776	Johns Island	CC	125-126
Arnold, William	26 Jul 1760		T	42
Arnold, Wm Senior	4 Jan 1758	Johns Island	S	240-242
Arthur, Nathaniel	8 Mar 1764		W	48-49
Arthur, Priscilla	29 Jan 1778		CC	339
Ash, Algernoon	9 Jan 1747/8		MM	242-243
Ash, Cato	9 Apr 1757		S	77-81
Ash, Cato			BB	9-10
Ash, James	9 Apr 1757		S	81-82
Ash, James	25 Apr 1766		X	208-209
Ash, James	9 Nov 1772	St. Pauls Parish, Chas. Town	Z	265
Ash, Joseph	16 Jul 1766		W	214-216
Ash, Richard Senr.	25 Sep 1766		W	316-317
Ash, Richard Cochran			S	194-196
Ash, Richard Cochn.	6 Jun 1770	Colleton Co.	Y	288-292
Ash, Theodora	14 May 1770		Y	237
Ash, Miss Theodora	6 Nov 1771	Beaufort, Port Royal	Z	132-133
Ashburn, Benj.	13 May 1750		B	407
Ashby, John	20 Jun 1758		T	11-17
Ashby, John	11 Jul 1764		W	174-175
Ashby, Thomas			R(2)	211-213
Ashby, Col. Thomas	24 Jan 1750/1		B	369-374
Asline, John	25 Oct 1763	Charles Town	V	534-541
Atchison, Jonah	14 Jun 1771	George Town	Z	22-23
Atchison, Jonah	4 Jul 1771	Georgetown	Z	43-46
Athal, John	16 Nov 1761		V	71
Atkin, Jean	15 Jan 1771		Y	367

Name	Date	Location	Vol. & pages
Atkins, Edmund	23 Jan 1762		V 131-134
Atkins, James	4 Feb 1774	St. Bartholomews Parish, Charles Town District	Z 484-486
Atkins, John	1 Aug 1770		Y 363-364
Atkins, Thomas	26 Mar 1750/1		B 434
Atkins, Thos.	15 May 1751	Beaufort	B 448-449
Atkinson, Anthony	3 Jun 1750		B 268-269
Atkinson, George	10 Aug 1773		& 299-300
Atkinson, George			CC 15
Atkinson, James	28 Mar 1771	Charlestown	Y 427
Atwell, Joseph	1 Jul 1772		& 135-136
Aubrey, Henry	10 May 1762		V 252-253
Audebert, Moses	1 May 1765	Charles Town	X 34-36
Audeburt, Moses	1 Jun 1769		Y 104
August, John	28 Jul 1774		& 428
Austin, Bartholomew	12 Jun 1771		Z 17-19
Austin, George	16 Nov 1774	Charlestown	AA 42-51
Austin, William	18 Sep 1777		CC 309-310
Avant, John	16 Apr 1750		R(1) 383-385
Avant, John			T 400
Avantt, Hannah	15 Feb 1777		AA 178
Averit, John Albright	22 Jan 1778	Orangeburgh Dist.	CC 352-354
Axson, Jacob Senr	26 Sept 1774		& 446
Ayres, Maurice	12 Apr 1769	Beaufort	X 445
Bachler, Ezekiel Senr.	29 Dec 1776		AA 212-213
Backhouse, Benjamin	21 & 22 Sep 1767	Charles Town	X 176-180
Backhouse, Benjamin	26 Dec 1767	Charles Town	X 223-229
Backhouse, Catherine	26 Dec 1767	Charles Town	X 222-223
Bacon, Jos.	30 Mar 1752		R(1) 330
Bacon, Joseph	30 Mar 1752		R(1) 526
Bacon, Nathaniel	24 Feb 1762		T 477
Baerd, Joshua	8 Nov 1773		Z 446-447
Bagbey, James	3 Apr 1761		T 571-575
Bailey, Eliza.	1 Apr 1771		Y 427
Bailey, Henry	18 Jan 1765		W 234-236
Bailey, Mary	22 Feb 1750/1		B 396
Bailey, Mary	1 Apr 1771		Y 426
Bailey, Richard			X 48-49
Baily, Ralph	4 Mar 1768	Edisto Island	X 303-305
Baird, Jeremiah			X 181-182
Baker, Benja.	28 Mar 1749		B 85
Baker, Elihu			B 88-89
Baker, Elihu	12 Jan 1765		W 203-204
Baker, Frans.	1749		B 166-170
Baker, James	10 Jun 1755		R(2) 337-338
Baker, John	31 Oct 1761		V 59-60
Baker, Mrs. Mary	28 Jun 1760		T 335-337
Baker, Richard	20 Jan 1753	Ashley	R(1) 513-516
Baker, Richard	22 Nov 1752	Charles Town	R(1) 463-467
Baker, Capt. Richard	30 Nov 1752	Charles Town	R(1) 503-506
Baker, Richard	9 Dec 1769	Chas. Town	Y 161
Baker, Mrs. Sarah		St. Georges Parish	MM 137-138
Baker, Mrs. Sarah	19 Nov 1774		& 475-476
Baker, Thomas	14 Mar 1774		& 327-328
Baker, Virtue	12 Jul 1754	Charles Town	R(2) 243-245
Baker, William	11 Sept 1761		V 46-47
Bakers, Lewis	4 Apr 1772		& 70-71
Baldwin, George	25 Mar 1768		X 279
Ball, Davd:			V 325-326
Ball, Elias	28 Sept 1758		T 81-82
Ball, Elias	18 Feb 1769	Ashepoo	X 432-434
Ball, George	4 May 1754		R(2) 174-175
Ball, James	4 Jun 1774	St. Helena Parish	& 423-424
Ball, John Coming			W 198-202
Ball, John Coming	18 Apr 1765	St. John's Berkley Co.	X 1-18
Ball, Joseph Sr.	21 Jan 1770	Charlestown	Y 174
Ball, Judith	30 Dec 1772		& 185-186

Name	Date	Location	Vol. & pages	
Ball, Sampson	28 Apr 1753	South side Santee	R(2)	3-5
Ball, Sampson	11 Jul 1766		W	290-291
Ballantine, John	14 Jul 1752	Charles Town	R(1)	444-445
Ballantine, John	29 Aug 1764	Charles Town, St. Michael's Parish	W	179-180
Ballantine, Thomas	23 Nov 1762		V	322-323
Bampfield, William	3 & 9 Jun 1773		Z	375-381
Bampfield, William	22 May 1775	Charles Town	&	593-600
Banbury, Peter	2 Feb 1757		S	44-46
Banister, William	26 Apr 1775		AA	99-100
Banks, Jeremiah	4 Jul 1754		R(2)	231-232
Bankson, Andrew	12 Feb 1760		T	294-295
Baraque, Jacob		Purysburgh, St. Peter Parish	X	404
Barker, Charles Junr.	2 Apr 1756		R(2)	424
Barker, Charles Sr.	21 May 1755		R(2)	345-346
Barksdale, Charles	29 Dec 1757		S	340-342
Barkesdale, Mary			BB	146-147
Barlow, Susanna	17 Sep ----		T	240
Barnes, Edmund	17 Jan 1758		S	352-354
Barnes, Capt. James	6 Jun 1766		W	292
Barnes, John	28 Aug 1756		R(2)	521
Barnes, John	6 Oct 1769		Y	129-131
Barnett, Thomas	24 Jan 1763		V	347
Barns, John	15 Oct 1768	Indian Town, Prince Fredericks Parish	X	400
Barns, George	17 Oct 1771		&	7
Barns, Robert	19 Oct 1776		BB	9
Barnwell, Nathaniel Sr.	3-7 Jan 1778	Beaufort	CC	308-309
Baron, Alexander	3 Mar 1760		T	290-291
Barr, Allan	5 Jun 1766	Williamsburgh	W	331
Barr, Ambrose			Z	332
Barr, Gavin	12 Apr 1763		V	530-532
Barr, John	24 Apr 1761		T	538
Barr, William	29 Nov 1764	Craven Co.	W	202-203
Barron, Francis			B	326-328
Barron, Rev. Robert	30 Jun 1764		W	140-141
Barry, Joseph	21 Feb 1753	Charles Town	R(2)	89-90
Barsh, David			Z	399-400
Bartlam, John	3 Oct 1781		BB	214
Barton, John	10 June 1748		MM	325
Barton, Mrs. Mary	17 Nov 1776		AA	156
Barton, Mary	2 May 1777		CC	316-317
Barton, Thomas	11 Mar 1775		&	544
Barton, William Sr.	26 Jan 1769		X	422-423
Basden, James	23 Nov 1773		&	311
Baskins, John	25 Mar 1769	Granville Co., Long Canes Settlement	X	447
Basquins, Thos.	26 June 1770		Y	278
Bassnett, John	25 May 1761		T	625-627
Batcheler, David	3 Jun 1767		W	440-441
Battson, Isaac	27 Apr 1772		&	101-103
Baxter, John	15 Jul 1771	St. Georges Parish	Z	34
Bayly, Tong	3 Mar 1749/50	St. Georges Parish	B	258
Baynard, Elizabeth	7 Jul 1773		Z	374-375
Baynard, Joseph	6 Oct 1770	Edistoe Island	Y	324-326
Baynard, William	15 Apr 1773		&	246-248
Baynes, Mrs. Jane	14 Mar 1757		S	76-77
Beaird, George	18 Oct 1754		R(2)	262
Beaird, George	19 Oct 1754		R(2)	266
Beaird, James	9 Sept 1761		T	62-64
Beak, Samuel	24 Jul 1764		W	177
Beal, Edward	8 Feb 1769		X	447-448
Bealy, William	22 May 1761		T	634-635
Bear, John	21 Jan 1768		X	443
Beard, Christopher	24 Feb 1768	St. Bartholomew Parish, Colleton Co.	X	281
Beard, Margaret	10 Oct 1770		&	322
Bearman, Joseph	21 Nov 1751	Santee	R(1)	135

Name	Date	Location	Vol. & pages	
Bearman, Joseph	26 Feb 1768		X	260
Bearman, Mary			Y	223
Beasley, Jane	26 Mar 1777		BB	43
Beaty, Francis	21 Apr 1777		CC	164-167
Beaty, John	30 May 1762		V	228-229
Bebey, Anthony	10 May 1760		T	307-308
Beck, George Phillip	15 Sept 1761	Prince Williams Parish	V	44
Beckett, John	7 May 1774		&	429-432
Beckman, Henry	13 Nov 1753	Charles Town	R(2)	87-89
Bedggood, Revd. Nicholas	6 Aug 1774		AA	6-10
Bedingfield, Charles	24 Jun 1773		&	271-273
Bedon, George	4 Jan 1769	Charles Town	X	428-430
Bedon, Col. Richd.	17 Aug 1765		X	49-50
Bedon, Mrs. Ruth	11 Apr 1765		W	244-246
Bedon, Stephen	27 Apr 1771	James Island	Z	25
Bee, John	10 Jul 1749		B	137-138
Bee, Joseph	11 Nov 1757		S	233-237
Bee, Martha	15 June 1751		R(1)	25-26
Bee, William	23 Dec 1766		W	354-355
Beiler, Jacob	22 Sept 1770	Berkley Co., Amelia Township	Y	320-321
Belin, James	24 May 1751		R(1)	11-13
Bell, Andrew	21 Jan 1754	Beaufort Town, Granville Co.	R(2)	123-127
Bell, Daniel			BB	113
[Bell, Elizth.]	7 Oct 1769		Y	165-166
Bell, Patrick	11 Feb 1773		Z	315-316
Bell, Thomas	21 Sep 1771		Y	361
Bell, Thomas	25 Jun 1771		Z	39-40
Bell, Rev. Thomas	14 Dec 1758		S	97-100
Bell, William	12 Jan 1769	Granville Co., Beaufort	X	407
Bell, William	24 Aug 1773		&	297-299
Bellinger, -----	15 Nov 1755		R(2)	379
Bellinger, George	10 Nov 1755	St. Andrews Parish	R(2)	378
Bellinger, Wm.	22 Mar 1770		Y	227-228
Bellune, William	6 Dec 1774		AA	54b-56
Bender, George	30 Oct 1773		Z	421-423
Benet, Thomas			W	252-253
Benhart, John			S	426
Benison, Elizabeth			R(1)	52
Benison, Coll. George	30 Aug 1749		B	165
Benison, Coll. George	2 Aug 1751	Christ Church Parish	R(1)	54-55
Bennison, Richard	31 Jan 1758		S	285-286
Bennet, David	16 Jan 1748/9		B	29-30
Bennet, Thomas			X	265
Bennett, Thomas	16 Jun 1764		W	141-142
Bennett, Moses			CC	390
Bennett, William	5 Jul 1773		Z	386
Benoist, Mrs.	19 May 1756		R(2)	454-455
Benoist, Ceasar free Negro	9 Apr 1778		CC	407-408
Benoist, James	13 Sept 1755		R(2)	371-372
Benoist, John	23 Jul 1764		W	173
Benoist, Peter	6 Oct 1746	Craven Co.	MM	25-27
Benoist, Peter	29 Nov 1756	St. Stephens Parish	S	4
Benoist, Peter	27 Jun 1759	Charles Town	T	225-234
Benoist, Peter	22 Mar 1763	Charles Town	V	134-140
Bensky, Martin	23 May 1750		S	398-399
[Bent, Noah]	2 Aug 1774		&	425
Beresford, Richard	16 Sept 1772	Charles Town	Z	295-300
Berkley, Mrs. Margt.			S	149-150
Bernard, James	5 May 1775	Prince Fredericks Parish	&	557-558
Berrie, Jas.			MM	320-322
Bessitt, William	23 Fev 1754	Charles Town	R(2)	138-139
Betham, Revd. Robert	5 Nov 1757		MM	169-172
Betterson, Jonathan	30 Nov 1752		R(1)	480
Bettson, Jonathan	11 Dec 1758		T	91
Bigler, Barnard			AA	262-263
Bilney, John	8 Mar 1759		T	161-162

Name	Date	Location	Vol. & pages	
Binford, Dr. Bernard	12 Jan 1774		&	328-331
Bird, Richard	30 Nov 1762		W	251
Bird, Robert	13 Dec 1768		X	423
Birkmyer, Daniel	8 Aug 1774		&	462
Bishop, Henry	31 Mar 1767		W	421
Bissett, Catherine			V	277-278
Black, Christopher	13 May 1755		R(2)	348
Black, Joseph	12 Dec 1757		S	332-333
Blackburn, Revd. Benjamin	24 Apr 1776		CC	23
Blackburn, Revd. Benjamin	24 Apr 1776		CC	68-69
Blair, Wade	31 Oct 1763		V	516-521
Blake, Daniel	15 Feb 1781	Prince Williams Parish, Grenville Co.	BB	141-146
Blake, Joseph	15 Sept 1751	Newington	R(1)	112-125
Blake, Nathaniel	16 May 1750		B	290-291
Blake, Richard Junr	15 Jun 1774		&	418-419
Blamyer, Capt. John	27 Jul 1765	St. Pauls Parish	W	273-274
Blamyer, Mary widow		Charles Town	V	529
Bland, Lancelot	12 Mar. 1778		CC	404
Bland, Richard	18 Jun 1776		&	603-604
Bland, Richard	18 Jun 1776		CC	21-22
Bleakley, John	23 Dec 1748		B	26-27
Blythe, Thomas	5 Feb 1762	Prince Georges Parish	Y	39-42
Boardsman, John		Williamsburgh	Y	233
Bobbough, Wm Junr	7 May 1753		R(2)	16-17
Bochet, Anthony	11 Jun 1774		&	460-461
Bochet, Anthony		St. Thomas Parish	AA	160
Bochet, Peter	28 May 1772		Z	225-226
Bochet, Samuel		St. Thomas & St. Dennis Parish	Z	223
Boddington, George	1758		T	96-97
Bodell, Ann widow	11 Apr 1771	Charles Town	Y	435-436
Bodell, Leonard			X	380-381
Boggan, William	31 Jul 1762		V	251-252
Boggis, John			T	444
Boggs, Francis	30 Jul 1771	John's Island	Z	42-43
Boggs, Isble	22 Mar 1757		S	83
Boggs, James	3 Jan 1751		R(1)	175-176
Boggs, James	21-22 Mar 1757		S	82-83
Bogs, Isabel	7 Apr 1752		R(1)	349-350
Bohner, Godfrid	10 Feb 1774	Charles Town	&	345-346
Boisseau, David	30 Jun 1759		T	203-204
Boisseau, James	23 Feb 1750/1		B	419-420
Boisseau, James Junr.	25 May 1756		R(2)	467-468
Boisseau, Mrs. Jane	3 Apr 1765		W	236
Bolton, Edward	12 Jun 1765		X	32-33
Bolton, James	18 Jun 1777		CC	191-194
Bolton, Thomas	30 Jan 1764		W	20
Bond, Mrs. Constantia	31 May 1754		R(2)	260-261
Bond, Ed.	7 Apr 1751		B	447-448
Bond, Jacob	16 Dec 1766		X	142
Bonetheau, John	20 July 1757		S	162-164
Bonhoste, John	23 Mar 1746/7		MM	86-87
Bonhoste, Jonah	4 Dec 1773		Z	473-478
Bonneau, Anthony	26 Apr 1757	St. Thomas Parish	S	124-130
Bonneau, Anthony	22 Mar 1777	Prince Williams Parish	BB	68
Bonneau, Elias	14 Aug 1773		&	340
Bonneau, Henry			V	50-53
Bonneau, Henry	16 May 1776		CC	101-104
Bonneau, Jacob	19 Feb 1767		W	416-417
Bonneau, John Henry	19 Apr 1754		R(2)	199-200
Bonneau, Mrs. Margarett Henrietta	18 Jun 1761		V	9-10
Bonneau, Peter	26 Jan 1748/9		B	48-50
Bonneau, Peter	10 Mar 1753		R(2)	116-119
Bonneau, Peter	29 Aug 1774	Prince Georges Parish	AA	12; 14-15
Bonneau, William	22 Mar 1777	Prince Williams Parish	BB	69
Bonnet, Jacob	10 Aug 1758		T	49

Name	Date	Location	Vol. & pages	
Bonnor, Henry	20 Mar 1759		T	150-151
Bonny, Thomas	13 Dec 1754	Charles Town	R(2)	504-506
Bonny, Capt. Thoms.	5 Jul 1751		R(1)	30-31
Boomer, John	29 Sep 1780		BB	99-100
Boone, Anne			R(1)	161-162
Boone, Anne	14 Nov 1751		R(1)	276-278
Boone, James	26 May 1749	Chas Town	B	98-99
Boone, Mrs. Jane	21 Feb 1771		Y	394-395
Boone, Mrs. Jane			Y	397
Boone, John		Christ Church Parish	BB	35-36
Boone, Margaret	3 Jul 1758		S	424-425
Boone, Mary	28 Nov 1780	Christ Church Parish	BB	110
Boone, Sam	18 Mar 1767		W	432
Boone, Thos.	25 July 1750		B	296
Boone, Major William	4 May 1751	St. John's Parish, Colleton County	B	449-452
Boone, William	19 Dec 1771		Z	167-169
Booth, John	10 Dec 1765	Prince Fredericks Parish	W	287
Booth, Martha	22 Jan 1763		V	339-340
Boschi, Charles			B	226-227
Bosher, Thomas	24 Mar 1777		BB	74-75
Bossard, Henry	5 Sept 1771		Z	115-116
Bossard, Henry Sr.	18 Feb 1771		Y	401-403
Boswood, James	29 Jun 1756		R(2)	488
Boswood, James	3 Dec 1777	St. Bartholomews Parish	CC	258-259
Boswood, William	7 Jul 1758		T	32-33
Bothwell, John	8 Dec 1777		CC	337-338
Boura, Peter	23 Jul 1774	Charlestown	AA	24
Bourget, Daniel	7 Mar 1770	Charles Town	Y	209-210
Bourline, Joseph	16 May 1781	St. Mathews Parish	BB	182
Boutwell, Burtinhead	16 & 17 Oct 1766		W	328-330
Boutwell, Burtonhd.	3 Oct 1769	Craven Co.	Y	139-145
Bowen, Owen	24 Feb 1768		X	281-282
Bower, Patrick	5 Feb 1782	Charles Town	BB	241-242
Bowers, George	22 May 1777	Camden District	CC	232-233;234
Bowler, Charles	1 Dec 1766	Colleton Co.	W	350-352
Bowman, Doctor John	29 May 1764	Craven Co., St. Mark's Parish	W	102
Bowman, John	24 Dec 1771	St. Georges Parish	&	2-3
Bowman, Thomas Senior	26 & 27 Aug 1773		&	295-297
Bowman, Thomas Senr.	23 & 24 Jan 1775		AA	86-89
Bowrey, William	11 Apr 1765	Prince Williams Parish	W	252
Box, Thomas	28 Feb 1774		&	311-313
Boyd, James	26 Apr 1750		B	249-250
Boydin, Daniel	25 Oct 1776		AA	180-181
Boykin, William	30 Apr 1760	Wateree	T	326-330
Boynton, Moses	8 Dec 1777		CC	291-293
Bracewell, William	21 Jul 1772		&	135
Brackenbury, Chas.	Feb 1748/9	Charlestown	B	78
Bradley, James		Prince Fredercisk Parish	CC	40-41
Bradley, John	1754		R(2)	258
Bradley, Thomas	12 Dec 1775	St. Helena Parish	BB	19-20
Bradsheet, Ensign	28 Jun 1781	Charles Town	BB	213-214
Bradwell, Isaac	10 Apr 1768		X	324-325
Bradwell, Joseph			W	417
Bradwell, Nathanel	16 Jan 1753		R(1)	506-508
Bradwell, Thomas	14 Jan 1768		X	258-259
Bradberry, Thomas Junr.	6 Feb 1773		&	203-204
Braggin, William	7 Aug 1752		R(1)	432
Brailsford, Joseph			T	411-413
Brailsford, John	3 Mar 1752		R(1)	309
Brailsford, Morton	5 Dec 1760		T	453-454
Bramham, Timothy	14 May 1750		B	262
Brandford, Barnaby			S	35-37
Brandford, Ezekiel			CC	379-381
Branford, Ann	2 Apr 1760		T	296-298
Branford, Barnaby	26 Aug 1768	St. Georges Parish	X	381-382
Branford, Malachi	2 Apr 1760		T	299

Name	Date	Location	Vol. & pages	
Branford, William	16 Oct 1751		R(1)	131-134
Branford, William	8 Jun 1767		W	447-456
Braund, John	29 Nov 1770	Charles Town	Y	349
Bready, William	9 Jul 1768		X	360
Breazeal, Henry	30 Aug 1770	Hillsborough Township, Granville Co.	Y	323-324
Breed, Timothy	18 Feb 1768	Charles Town	X	278
Bremar, Francis	25 Jun 1760		T	330-337
Bremar, James	11 Nov 1749		B	187-192
Bremar, Martha	2 Jun 1769	Charles Town	Y	177-180
Bretton, Daniel infant	24 Jul 1751		R(1)	68
Bretton, Francis	17 Jul 1768		Y	380-381
Brewton, John	28 Aug 1777	Charles Town	AA	259-262
Brewton, Mary	16 Jan 1761		V	64
Brickett, Matthias	9 Dec 1771		&	8-9
Bridges, John Jacob	7 Oct 1746		MM	10-11
Brigle, Jacob	23 May 1771		Z	39
Brindley, Henry	9 Feb 1775		&	514
Brisbane, William	30 Jan 1772	Charles Town	&	16-17
Brisbane, William	7 June 1773		&	260
Brittain, William			T	307
Britton, Daniel	19 Jan 1749/50		B	219-220
Britton, Jane	17 July 1758		T	18
Britton, Joseph	18 May 1774		&	357-358
Britton, Moses	24 July 1750		B	439
Britton, Moses	24 May 1774		&	355-357
Britton, Phillip	7 Apr 1750		B	243-244
Britton, Timothy	20 Mar 1750/1		B	421
Broadbelt, Jane	25 May 1763		V	383-384
Broadbelt, John			W	275-276
Broadbelt, William	22 Mar 1757		S	118-120
Brockington, Sarah	30 Jan 1761		T	440
Brockinton, Daniel	19 Feb 1770		Y	200
Brockinton, Daniel	25 Apr 1772		Z	211
Brockinton, Joseph	1 Mar 1776			
Bromley, Thomas	7 Sep 1765	Charles Town	X	46-48
Brooks, Jacob	26 Apr 1774	Craven Co.	&	365-366
Broughton, Alexander		St. Johns, Berkley Co.	W	217-221
Broughton, Andrew	11 Nov 1771	Charles Town	Z	129
Broughton, Elizabeth	2 May 1757		S	138-139
Broughton, Hannah			T	484-486
Broughton, Nathaniel	8 Mar 1755		R(2)	313-315
Broughton, Nathaniel	6 Jan 1762	Chas Town	V	124-125
Broughton, Peter	31 May 1769		X	462-463
Broughton, Sarah			B	293
Broughton, Thomas	10 Feb 1752		R(1)	339-342
Broughton, Thomas			V	21-23
Broughton, Thomas	20 Jan 1764		W	15-17
Brown, David	10 Jun 1765	Charles town	X	40-41
Brown, Edwd.	6 Dec 1762		V	314
Brown, Elizabeth	18 Dec ----		T	100
Brown, Mrs. Elizabeth	21 Jul 1766		W	312
Brown, Geo.			S	357-359
Brown, Hugh	18 Feb 1775	Charlestown	&	526-528
Brown, John	25 Jan 1747/8	Charles Town	MM	289-290
Brown, John			Z	99
Brown, John			&	28-29
Brown, John	2 May 1777		BB	45
Brown, Capt. Joseph	10 Jul 1770	Charles Town	Y	350-351
Brown, Capt. Lazarus	19 Aug 1772		Z	255-256
Brown, Margaret	19 Dec 1777	St. Bartholomews Parish	CC	281-282
Brown, Mary	16 Mar 1772		&	69-70
Brown, Nicholas	25 Apr 1754		R(2)	181-182
Brown, Patrick	7 Nov 1755	Augusta, Georgia	R(2)	373-376
Brown, Dr. Robert			T	113-118
Brown, Robert	19 Jun 1773		&	265-266
Brown, Talbott	21 Aug 1746	Charles Town	MM	8-10
Brown, Thomas	16-28 July 1746/7	Saxe Gotha	MM	162-169

Name	Date	Location	Vol. & pages	
Brown, Thomas	11 Jul 1748	Congrees	B	12
Brown, Thomas			B	344-346
Brown, William			B	217-218
Brown, William	8 May 1764		W	101-102
Brown, William	31 Oct 1766		W	331-332
Brown, William	27 June 1768		X	375
Brown, Capt. William	24 Jul 1756		R(2)	491
Browne, Alexander	22 May 1750	George Town	B	305-308
Browne, Francis	10 Mar 1754		R(2)	194-197
Bruce, John	20 July 1750		B	283-284
Bruce, John	5 Jul 1765		X	37-38
Bruce, Samuel	3 Oct 1774	St. Stephens Parish, Santee	AA	29
Bruce, Dr. William	26 May 1752		R(1)	426-431
Bruneau, Paul	24 Aug 1758		T	78-80
Brunet, Esaie	22 Nov 1757	Charles Town	S	306-308
Brunett, Esaic	9 Mar 1761	Charlestown	V	445-447
Brunett, Mrs. Susannah Mary	7 Jul 1760	Charles Town	T	346-349
Brunson, Isaac	15 Oct 1770		Y	327-328
Brunson, James Sr.	9 Jan 1771		Y	368-369
Brunson, John & Abigail			R(1)	399-400
Brunson, John Senr.		Charles Town	R(2)	508
Brunson, Josiah			T	392
Brunson, Thomas	6 Nov 1749		B	178
Brunston, Abraham			B	26
Bryan, Hugh	12 Mar 1754	Granville Co.	R(2)	153-156
Bryan, Hugh	19 Jul 1760		T	359
Bryan, James			BB	222
Bryan, John	15 Dec 1763		V	508
Bryan, John	28 Dec 1772	Charles Town	&	204
Bryan, Joseph	13 Jan 1736/7	Granville Co.	R(2)	401-402
Bryan, Joseph	7 Feb 1752	Prince William Parish, Granville Co.	R(1)	353-355
Bryan, Joseph Junr.	2 Dec 1756	Prince William	S	4-6
Bryant, Nicholas	10 Mar 1765	Santee	W	236-237
Brynan, John	22 Dec 1774	Red Bluff, Peedee	&	524
Buchanan, John	2 Dec 1755		R(2)	408
Buchanan, William	20 Apr 1757		S	133-136
Buchanan, William		Combahee	T	210-213
Buchannan, William	1 Sept 1758		T	55-61
Buckholt, Anthony	8 Nov 1777		CC	266
Buckholts, Henry	27 Apr 1767		X	92-93
Buckner, Thomas			X	23
Budding, John			R(2)	269
Buer, Thos.			Y	326-327
Bull, Barnaby	14 Mar 1755		R(2)	328-329
Bull, Mrs. Mary	16 Jan 1772	Euhaws	Z	177-187
Bull, Stephen	26 Apr 1751		B	356
Bull, Stephen	28 Feb 1770	Prince Williams Parish	Y	228-229
Bull, Capt. Thomas	1 Feb 1773		&	210-212
Bull, Capt. Thomas	22 Fev 1775	Willton	AA	72-74
Bull, William Lt. Gov	17 Jun 1755	Granville Co.; St. Andrews Parish	R(2)	349-351
Bullard, Edward	9 Apr 1767		W	415-416
Bulline, John	7 May 1772		&	86-89
Bulline, Thomas		St. James, Goose Creek	B	397-398
Bulline, Thomas	8 Jul 1768		X	358
Bulline, Thomas	24 Nov 1769		Y	208-209
Burd, Mrs. Elizabeth	3 June 1768		X	369-371
Burd, William	9 & 10 Feb 1759	Edisto	T	162-166
Burdeaux, James	2 Jul 1767		X	93-94
Burden, James	26 Jun 1777		CC	199
Burgess, John			Z	364-365
Burgess, John	10 Jun 1774	Charles Town	&	378
Burgess, John		Waccamaw, Prince George Parish	CC	233-234
Burgess, Joseph	18 Jul 1751		R(1)	51
Burgess, Sarah	11 Feb 1769		X	431

Name	Date	Location	Vol. & pages	
Burn, John	17 Jul 1775		&	576-583
Burn, Samuel	2 Dec 1773		Z	453-454
Burne, James	22 May 1775		CC	48-49
Burnet, Daniel			R(1)	93
Burnet, Henry			V	60
Burnet, John	18 May 1776		CC	6-7
Burnett, Dr. Andrew	13 Jun 1765	Black Mingo	W	259-260
Burnett, Mary			V	230-232
Burnham, Benjamin	25 Apr 1761		T	619-620
Burnham, Nicho.	29 May 1747		MM	133
Burnham, Thomas	14 Feb ----		T	129-130
Burnley, Thomas	2 Nov 1747		MM	212-214
Burnley, William	22 May 1750		B	291-292
Burns, John	18 Mar 1775	Black Mingo	&	523-524
Burton, Benjamin	18 Apr 1764	St. Helena's Parish	W	56
Burton, Richard	24 Apr 1763	St. Phillips Parish	V	369-372
Burton, Samuel & Mary	12 Nov 1761		T	235
Burton, Thomas	11 June 1756	Granville Co.	R(2)	486
Burton, Thomas	23 Feb 1757		S	32-33
Burton, Thos.	5 Sep 1774	Pedee	AA	23-24
Bush, Edward	14 July 1769		Y	319
Bush, Peter	2 Mar 1771		Y	425-426
Bushell, William	28 Oct 1776		AA	146-147
Buss, William Litton	24 Jan 1764		W	33-35
Bussey, George	18 Nov 1765		X	182-184
Butler, Charles	31 Oct 1752		R(1)	453-455
Butler, Charles	7 & 10 Oct 1774		&	451-452
Butler, Mrs. Elizth.	27 Mar 1771		Y	436-437
Butler, George	26 May 1750		B	275-276
Butler, James	2 Jan 1761		T	470
Butler, James	20 Feb 1777		AA	215
Butler, Mary			R(1)	391-392
Butler, Peter	30 Nov 1767	Charles Town	X	235-236
Butler, Samuel	13 Jun 1767		X	77-78
Butler, Thomas	Mar 1746/7	Prince William Parish	MM	134-136
Butler, William	6 Apr 1754		R(2)	203-208
Butler, William			W	195
Buttler, Capt. John	15 Oct 1763		V	504
Byers, Joseph	23 Dec 1777		CC	319
Byers, Robert	Dec 1776		AA	253
Cabanis, Jane			T	325
Cacker, Bryent	11 Jan 1771		Y	420-421
Cahusac, John	21 May 1761		T	622-624
Caine, G.	3 Mar 1781		BB	114
Calcole, James	4 Aug 1777		CC	219-220
Calder, Archibald	25 Mar 1752		R(1)	374-379
Calder, Archibald	20 May 1777		CC	185-191
Calder, John			W	385-389
Calhoun, Ezekiel	21 Sep 1762	Granville Co.	V	270-271
Calhoun, Patrick	5 Sep 1777	Ninety Six District	CC	295
Callaghan, John	15 & 16 May 1781		BB	186-188
Callihorn, Dennis	23 May 1748		MM	319
Cambell, James	20 Aug 1766		W	309
Cameron, Alexr.	4 Nov 1776	St. Marks Parish	BB	12
Camlin, William	24 Mar 1774		&	318
Camlin, William	25 Mar 1774		&	321
Campbell, Alexander	8 Oct 1766		W	322-323
Campbell, Catherine	27 Apr 1773		&	243
Campbell, Colin	24 Apr 1777		BB	41
Campbell, Dougal	28 Dec 1770		Y	386-391
Campbell, Mathew	28 Nov 176-		T	427
Campbell, Samuel	2 Aug 1773	Charles Town	&	292
Campbell, William	24 Mar 1769		X	438
Camplin, William	27 Mar 1770		Y	214
Cannon, John	17 Jun 1763		V	470-472
Cantey, Joseph	27 Feb 1764	St. Mark's Parish, Craven County	W	23

Name	Date	Location	Vol. & pages	
Cantey, Joseph & Josiah	27 Feb 1764	St. Mark's Parish	W	22
Cantey, Saml.	17 Oct 1763		V	525
Cantey, Samuel	13 Mar 1777	St. Mark's Parish	BB	37-39
Cantly, John	10 Jul 1761		V	87
Canty, Josiah	2 Feb 1774		Z	491-493
Cantzon, John	13 Dec 1773		Z	472-473
Cape, Dr. Jonathan			W	356-357
Capers, Richard	28 Apr 1755		R(2)	361-362
Capers, Richard	9 & 10 May 1774	Christ Church Parish	&	350-352
Capers, Richard Jr.	22 Dec 1762		V	360
Capers, Thomas	9 June 1767		W	443
Cardy, Samuel	16 Mar 1774		&	319-320
Carey, William	31 Jul 1747		MM	158
Cargill, John	7 Jan 1771	Chas. Town	Y	361
Carlile, James	15 Aug 1772		&	126-128
Carne, Samuel	6 Feb 1768		X	256-257
Carne, Samuel	3 Mar 1768		X	327-328
Carney, James	30 Apr 176-	Amelia Town Ship	V	240
Carpenter, Abia	18 Jul 1768		X	285-286
Carpenter, George	27 Jan 1767		W	368-370
Carrel, Patrick			T	426-427
Carroll, Charles	25 Aug 1752		R(1)	436-437
Carroll, Charles	23 Jan 1755	Charles Town	R(2)	277-278
Carruthies, Willm.	21 Sept 1771		Z	372-373
Carson, Dr. James	17 Dec 1777	Wadmelah, St. John's Parish	CC	302-305
Carson, Samuel			V	19-20
Carson, William	30 Dec 1777		CC	400
Carss, William	3 Nov 1777		CC	366-368
Cart, Thomas		St. Phillips Parish	R(2)	424
Cartwright, Hugh	13 Oct 1753		R(2)	90-93
Cartwright, William	21 Jun 1768	Colleton Co.	X	387
Carwithin, William	26 Oct 1770	Charles Town	Y	341-342
Carwithin, William	22 Dec 1770		&	550
Cary, John	9 Mar 1761		T	476
Case, [William]	6 Dec 1777		CC	301-302
Caser, Doctor	21 Aug 1754		R(2)	169
Cass, Jacob			T	80-81
Cater, Benjamin	20 May 1751		B	448
Cater, Thos.	5 Oct 1753	St. George's Parish	R(2)	75-78
Cater, Wm.	8 Dec 1749		B	204-205
Caterton, Wm.	21 Dec 1776		CC	122-123
Cathcart, James	22 May 1762	Granvel Co.	V	205-206
Cathcart, William			R(2)	210
Cattel, Charles	20 May 1758		T	109-111
Cattell, John	29 Apr 1769	St. Georges Parish	Y	60-62
Cattell, John	13 & 14 Apr 1774		&	360-364
Cattell, John	1 Sep 1758		T	51-53
[Cattell], Peter Jr.	24 May 1748		MM	330
Cattell, Mrs. Sarah	15 Dec 1766		W	390-391
Cattell, William	16 Nov 1752		R(1)	491-500
Cattell, William Junr		Charles Town	R(1)	153-157
Caw, David	4 Apr 1759		T	185-189
Caw, David	20 Oct 1761		V	12-19
Caw, David	20 Jun 1767	Charles Town	W	457-459
Caw, David			W	38-43
Caw, David	22 May 1770	Charles Town	Y	251-255
Caw, Dr. Thomas	8 Mar 1773	Charles Town	Z	343-350
Cawel, William	16 Nov 1759		T	322-323
Chalmers, James			W	350
Chalmers, Lionel	7 Jul 1777	Charles Town	BB	75-84
Chalmers, William	19 Nov 1755		R(2)	398
Chamberlain, Joseph	29 Jan 1754	Craven Co.	R(2)	109
Chambers, James	26 Feb 1755		R(2)	329-330
Chambers, James	20 Apr 1762		V	176
Champignie, Peter	30 May 1751		B	453-454
Champneys, John			R(1)	58-61
[Chandler, Elizabeth]			AA	173-174
Chandler, Isaac	27 Feb 1749/50	St. Georges Parish, Berkley Co.	B	233-235

11

Name	Date	Location	Vol. & pages	
Chandler, Robert	1 Mar 1775		AA	84-86
Changler, Samuel	2 Jan 1778		CC	319-320
Chaplin, Benjamin	13 Jul 1768		X	362-363
Chaplin, John	3 Oct 1776		CC	110-112
Chaplin, Will			T	418-419
Chapman, [Ann]	Aug 1747		MM	158-161
Chapman, John	14 Dec 1776		&	642
Chapman, John	13 Feb 1770	Charles Town	Y	214-216
Chapman, Sarah	24 Jun 1754		R(2)	220
Chapman, Thos.			Z	139
Chapman, William	24 May 1751		B	455-457
Chapman, William		James Island, St. Andrews Parish	CC	392-394
Chardonnet, Abraham		Purrysburgh, St. Peters Parish	MM	318
Chastaingu, Theodore	13 Mar 1749/50		B	267-268
Cheesborough, Elizabeth			T	584
Chesdine, Alexander	2 Dec 1772	Christ Church Parish	&	173-174
Chesnut, James	21 Oct 1773		Z	400
Chevillette, John	23 May 1771		Z	75-77
Chicken, John	16 Nov 1774	St. James, Santee	&	470
Chicken, Wm	19 Mar 1778	St. James Parish, Santee	CC	412-413
Chiffell, Henry			T	138-139
Chiffell, Rev. Mr. Henry	20 Jul 1757		T	271-272
Child, Anne	17 Nov 1768		X	423
Chineys, David	24 Dec 1767	Granville Co.	X	263-264
[Chinner, Thomas]	11 Apr 1755		W	262
Chinners, Abraham	11 Jun 1759		T	200-201
Chinners, Isaac	28 Jun 1766		W	341-342
Chisholme, William	25 Feb 1782	Charles Town	BB	244
Chopard, Danl.	23 Aug 1770	Charles Town	Y	306-307
Chovin, [Alexander]	20 Nov 1756		S	19-21
Chovin, Isaac	20 Aug 1754	Craven Co., St. James Santee	R(2)	237-238
Christie, Alexander	15 Jan 1757		S	40-41
Christie, Henry	4 May 1775		&	551
Christie, Dr. James	21 Aug 1762		V	267-270
Christie, Dr. James	14 Sept 1767		X	166
Christie, Jean	14 Sept 1767		X	167
Christy, Hugh			T	380
Chubb, James			Y	417
Clagg, Samuel	25 Jul 1749		B	150
Clancey, John	15 Jun 1759		T	215
Clancey, John	21 Nov 1762		V	300-301
Clapp, Eliza.	21 Jun 1751	Charles Town; Sante	R(1)	111-112
Clark, Archibald	2 Aug 1777		AA	253-254
Clark, Edward	6 Sep 1749		B	163
Clark, Edwd.	14 Apr 1769	St. Davids Parish	X	459
Clark, George			R(2)	357
Clark, George			R(2)	390
Clark, James Lardent	26 Feb 1773		&	223-226
Clark, Jeremiah	16 Mar 1749/50		B	274-275
Clark, John			B	350-351
Clark, John	18 Aug 1768	All Saints Parish	X	378
Clark, John	21 Oct 1772	Prince George Parish, Craven Co.	&	169
Clark, John	15 May 1777	Charles Town	BB	42
Clark, Robert			&	230-231
Clark, Samuel	4 Dec 1746		R(1)	458-462
Clark, Saml.	3 Jan 1778		CC	314
Clark, Samuel	23 Mar 1746/7		MM	83-84
Clark, Samuel	14 Nov 1746		MM	53-54
Clark, Thos.	26 Feb 1746/7		MM	86
Clarke, Benjamin	20 Jan 1778	Beaufort, St. Helena Parish	CC	318-319
Clarke, James	25 Apr 1768		X	347-348
Clarke, Samuel	27 Dec 1776		BB	12-13
Clarkson, Doctr. William	25 Jan 1777		AA	181-182
Clase, Martha	23 Sept 1769		Y	155
Claudy, Valantine			W	277

Name	Date	Location	Vol. & pages	
Clayton, John	7 Nov 1771		Z	157-161
Clayton, John	26 Mar 1773		&	257
Clayton, John	25 Jun 1771		Z	26-27
Clayton, Sarah	15 Feb 1772	St. Georges Parish	Z	171
Clayton, Sarah (widow)	7 May 1772		&	52-53
Cleator, John	9 Oct 1770		Y	368
Cleave, Nathan	29 Aug 1764	St. Thomas Parish	W	147-149
Cleeland, Dr. John	27 Feb 1764	Charles Town	W	42-45
Cleiland, Willm.	28 May 1762		V	227
Cleland, Hon. John	15 Jul 1760	George Town	T	352-358
Clement, Daniel	3 Aug 1763		V	477-478
Clement, William	29 Nov 1766		W	362-363
Clemmons, Benjamin	18 Mar 1772		&	30-31
Clemmons, Robert	8 May 1769		Y	89-90
Clerk, James	20 Jul 1750		B	315-317
Clifford, John	1 May 1765	Charlestown	X	28-30
Clifford, Sarah	27 Jan 1759		T	167-168
Clifford, Thomas	13 Aug 1762	St. Bartholomews Parish	V	254-261
Clifford, Thomas Junr	23 Sep 1767		X	175-176
Clifford, William	13 Mar 1745/6		MM	152-155
Cliffs, Thomas	27 Apr 1782		BB	255
Clunie, John	25 Nov 1772		&	190
Clyatt, Samuel	27 Sept 1753		R(2)	65
Coachman, John	6 Apr 1750		B	251-252
Coachman, William	1 May 1770	Prince George, Winyaw	Y	246-249
Coats, Wm.	25 Jul 1781		BB	205
Cochran, Hugh	28 --- 1756		R(2)	438-439
Cochran, Dr. John	13 May 1763		V	377-380
Cochran, Michael	20 Jun 1769		Y	127-129
Cochran, William	22 Dec 1757	St. Bartholomew's Parish	S	262-263
Cockrield, Barnaby	21 Feb 1771		Y	404-405
Cockfield, John	18 Oct 1762		V	290-291
Codner, Charles	19 Oct 1747	Charles Town	MM	200-201
Coffey, Marian widow	30 Nov 1757	Charles Town	S	220-221
Cogdell, Charles	24 & 25 Sept 1776		&	617-618
Coke, Joseph	6 Jan 1747/8	Johns Island	MM	255-257
Colcock, Elizabeth			X	221-222
Colcock, Isaac	28 Jan 1767		X	129-130
Colcoke, John	1 Mar 1757	Charles Town	S	47-48
Cole, James	8 Jun 1750	Charlestown	B	302
Cole, John	1 Sep 1758		T	43-45
Cole, Mark	28 May 1771		Z	40
Cole, Mary	31 May 1757	Johns Island	S	167-169
Cole, Richard			Y	318
Cole, Thomas	3 Dec 1771		&	7-8
Cole, William	6 Oct 1761		V	58
Coleman, Richard			Y	318
Coleman, Thomas	27 Jun 1769	Charles Town	Y	236
Collans, Peter			CC	204-206
Colleton, John	27 Nov 1751	Berkley Co.	R(1)	142-152
Colleton, Hon. John	8 Sep 1750		B	332-334
Colleton, Sir John	5 Dec 1780		BB	123-126
Colleton, Sir John			BB	255
Colleton, Sir John	30 Dec 1777	Charles Town District	CC	267-273
Collier, John	20 July 1754		R(2)	257
Collier, John	16 Nov 1754		R(2)	333
Collings, Jona.		St. Thomas Parish	V	84
Collings, Mary	29 Mar 1774	St. Thomas Parish	Z	532-533
Collins, Daniel			MM	273-274
Collins, John	10 Dec 1769		Y	171-172
Collins, Jonah	30 May 1749	Craven Co.	B	142-147
Collins, Jonah	26 Apr 1750		R(2)	406
Collins, Robt	30 May 1758		S	404-407
Collins, Mrs. Sarah	15 Mar 1762	Christ Church Parish	V	140-141
Colson, Abraham	19 May 1750	Craven Co.	B	328-330
Colson, Abraham	18 Jul 1752		R(1)	480
Colvett, Peter	16 Nov 1758	Chas. Town	T	90
Comb, Thomas	18 May 1774	Charles Town	&	377-378

Name	Date	Location	Vol. & pages	
Combe, Paul	1 Dec 1766		W	376-377
Combe, Philip	18 May 1772		&	61
Comber, Thomas	29 Jun 1774		&	414-415
Commander, George			W	181
Commander, Joseph	15 Jun 1772		Z	234-236
Commeralt, George	2 Oct 1764		W	181-182
Conn, Thomas	7 Apr 1768		X	348-349
Conner, John Junr.		Colleton Co.	&	530-531
Connor, John	13 Dec 1767	Prince Williams Parish	X	219-220
Connor, John	19 Jul 177-		CC	400
Cook, Isaac	25 Jun 1772		Z	241-245
Cook, Jeremiah	23 Nov 1749		B	206
Cook, John	11 Oct 1766		W	345
[Cook, John]	8 Jun 1774		&	392
Cook, Samuel	25 Jul 1777		CC	243-244
Coomer, William	6 Mar 1771		Z	13
Coon, William	9 Nov 1760		T	379-380
Cooner, Francis			T	408-409
Cooper, George	11 Oct 1759	Indian Town	T	262a-262
Cooper, Jacob	6 Dec 1769	Craven Co.	Y	167
Cooper, John	24 Dec 1766	Stono	X	148-158
Cooper, John	29 Jan 1771		Y	379-380
Cooper, Samuel	17 May 1774	Prince Frederick Parish, Craven Co.	&	370-371
Cooper, Thomas	1 Sep 1772		Z	257-259
Cooper, James	9 Jan 1772	Craven Co., Prince Frederick Parish	Z	167
Coram, Edward	1 May 1762		V	159
Corbans, Peter	28 Jun 1777		AA	238-239
Cordes, Charles	28 Mar 1775		&	525-526
Cordes, Henrietta Catherine			W	221-222
Cordes, James Paul			BB	17
Cordes, Thomas			V	492-494
Cordes, Col. Thomas			B	124-129
Cords, John	2 Jan 1757		S	22-28
Corker, Thomas	-- Feb 1771		Z	1-12
Cormack, Alexander	4 Nov 1773		Z	435-441
Cornwell, George	22 Apr 1768		X	295
Corse, Timothy Hanson	3 Mar 1774		&	314-315
Cossens, Edmund			CC	293-295
Cosslett, Charles Matthews	22 Oct 1776	Charlestown	AA	164-165
Cotes, Rev. Mr.	20 Dec 1752		R(1)	475-476
Cotterell, Capt. John	5 May 1763		V	473
Coulliette, Christopher	2 Apr 1772		&	34
[Coulliette, Thomas]	25 Aug 1764		W	177-178
Coulliette, Mrs. Mary	30 May 1764		W	126-128
Counsell, Jesse	10 Dec 1774		AA	51-53a
Counsell, Robert	4 Jul 1768		X	354-355
County, William	21 Feb 1748/9		B	96
Courtonne, Jerome	6 Mar 1762		V	122-123
Coushet, Andrew	2 Jun 1750		B	292-293
[Coustiel, Alexander]	21 Mar 1765		W	247
Couterie, Daniel	25 Aug 1748		B	225
Couterier, Elias	16 Jul 1765	Prince Williams Parish	W	269
Couterier, Francis			T	10-11
Couterier, Gideon	29 Nov 1756	St. Stephens Parish	R(2)	557-558
Cowen, Bemer			Y	350
Cowen, Benjamin	9 May 1759		T	195-196
Cowen, Benjamin			V	141
Cowen, John	27 Aug 1752		R(1)	441-444
Cowen, Mary			W	18
Cowen, Thomas	19 Apr 1773		&	249-250
Cowley, James	15 May 1747		MM	98
Cox, John			R(1)	372-373
Cox, Joseph	25 May 1761		T	630-632
Coyle, Thomas	10 Apr 1762		V	185
Coyt, Hercules	2 Jul 1750		B	284-285

Name	Date	Location	Vol. & pages	
Crafford, James Senr.	17 Sep 1777		CC	235-236
Crawford, Daniel	11 Jul 1760		T	366-379
Crawford, David	7 Jan 1764	Granville Co.	W	12-13
Crawford, Hugh	21 Aug 1762		V	212-262
Crawford, John	7 Jan 1747/8		MM	256
Crawford, John	21 Apr 1761		T	584-586
Crawford, John	5 Nov 1771		Z	138
Cree, David	7 Jan 1767		X	159-160
Creek, Henry	5 Apr 1775		AA	82
Creese, Mathew	1 Jul 1748		MM	331-332
Cregg, John	23 Sep 1776	Black Mingo, Prince Fredericks Parish	&	609-610
Crell, Stephen	22 Jul 1763		W	15
Crim, Peter	24 Jan 1761		T	439-440
Cripps, Robert			&	321-324
Croft, Mrs. Catherine	7 Apr 1769	Santee	X	441-442
Croft, Childermas	30 Nov 1761	Charles Town	V	89-90
Croft, Edward	1 Sep 1756	Christ Church Parish	R(2)	531-532
Croft, John	7 Jan 1762		V	85-86
Croft, John	23 Jan 1773	Prince George Parish	&	192
Croft, Robert	19 Nov 1776	George Town District, Santee	AA	157-160
Crofts, Miss Sarah			&	546-547
Crokatt, John & Kenneth Michie	3 Mar 1760		T	289-291
Crokatt, Dr. James	29 Oct 1765		Y	13-18
Croll, Archibald	22 Jul 1758		T	19
Croll, Mrs. Catherine	30 Oct 1772	St. Pauls Parish	&	165-166
Cromer, William		Charles Town	R(2)	108-109
Crook, William			T	404-406
Crooks, Benjamin	3 Feb 1746/7		MM	70
Crosby, Dennis	1 Jan 1772	Craven Co.	&	4-6
Cross, John			T	292
Crossky, William	16 Jun 1752		R(1)	392-393
Crossler, John	14 Feb 1750/1		B	400
Crosswell, Benjamin	23 Jun 1750		B	283
Crosthwaite, Mary	28 Jun 1760		V	191-192
Crosthwaite, Thomas	24 Aug 1756	Charles Town	R(2)	526-528
Crosthwaite, William Ward	23 Apr 1770	Prince Williams Parish	Y	263-267
Crosthwaite, William Ward			CC	202-204
Crouch, Abraham	23 Dec 1763		W	6-7
Crouch, Charles		Charlestown	AA	239-241
Culley, Jas.			Y	377
Culliatt, Adam	25 Nov 1768		X	426-427
Cullyer, Thomas			W	355-356
Culp, Casper	16 Jul 1770	Craven Co.	Y	299
Culp, Philip Senr	9 Feb 1778		CC	419-420
Cumbe, John	12 Aug 1771	St. Thomas Parish	Z	43
Cummicks, Michael			T	135-136
Cumming, Benjamin	19 Aug 1776		&	615
Cumming, Rev. Robt.	13 Jan 1752		R(1)	279-282
Cunning, William	2 Jun 1748		MM	317-318
Curron, Thomas	16 Apr 1752	Williamsburg	R(1)	441
Cussens, John			R(1)	82-83
Cussings, George	25 Aug 1754		R(2)	176-177
Cuttino, Jacob		Prince Georges Parish	R(2)	296
Cuttino, Peter	1 Sep 1766		X	56
Cuttinoe, Joll	-- Sep 1759		T	238-239
Cyrus free Negro			&	335
Dale, Oliver	17 Sep 1774		AA	21-23
Dale, Dr. Thomas			R(2)	369-370
Dall--, Capt. Hugh	31 Aug 1769		Y	112
Dallas, Francis	3 Apr 1759		T	197-198
Dalrymple, Thomas	4 May 1774	Ninety Six District	&	378-379
Dalton, Catherine			R(2)	66
Dalton, Charles	9 Feb 1775	St. Bartholomews Parish, Colleton Co.	&	502

Name	Date	Location	Vol. & pages	
Dalton, Daniel	29 Jul 1758		T	36-37
Dalton, Willm.	14 Jun 1758		S	413-416
Dalton, Wm. Jr.	26 Apr 1755		R(2)	327
Daly, Daniel	3 May 1755	St. Helena's Parish, Granville Co.	R(2)	347-348
Daly, Daniel	1 Jan 1758		T	92-93
Dandridge, Francis	24 Apr 1758		S	360-361
Danford, John	11 Apr 1775		&	554
Daniell, John	2 Dec 1747	Charles Town	MM	217-227
Dannally, Brian	21 Nov 1777		CC	311
Danner, John	7 Feb 1777		AA	213
Dalton, James	10 Nov 1746		MM	40-42
Dandridge, William	13 Aug 1768		X	371-373
Darby, James	23 Dec 1773		Z	435
Darby, Mrs. Margaret	11 Sep 1777		AA	257-258
Dargan, John	12 Aug 1766		W	323-324
Darquier, Moses			Z	58-64
Darrel, Joseph	18 Jan 1781		BB	167-168
Dart, John	11 Feb 1755	Charles Town	R(2)	297-307
Darvil, Elizabeth			W	216-217
Darvill, Ebsworth	14 Jul 1747		MM	156-158
Dash, William	6 Feb 1769		Y	36
Davant, Isaac			AA	145-146
David, Ezekiel	14 Nov 1768		X	410-411
David, Owen	14 Jul 1770	St. Davids Parish	Y	357-358
David, Peter	20 May 1754		R(2)	192-194
Davidson, Alexander	30 Oct 1766		W	345-347
Davidson, Alexander	4 Jun 1770		Y	293-294
Davidson, Samuel	22 Aug 1755		R(2)	360-361
Davidson, Susanna			V	109-110
Davidson, Thomas	10 Sep 1764		W	176
Davis, Ann	29 Mar 1760		B	231
Davis, Capt. David	8 Jan 1772		Z	187-189
Davis, George	21 Feb 1772	St. Michaels Parish, Charlestown	Z	207-208
Davis, James	12 Oct 1768		X	391-392
Davis, Joseph			T	76
Davis, Samuel	26 Jul 1775	Granville Co.	AA	153
Davis, William	11 Sep 1773		Z	389
Dawson, Charles	10 Feb 1781	Charles Town	BB	189-190
Dawson, Rev. William	18 Jan 1769	Charlestown	X	413
Day, Thomas	20 Dec 1764	Charles Town	W	210-215
Day, Doctor William	21 Apr 1774		&	347-350
Day, Doctr. William	8 Aug 1777		A	251-252
Dean, Daniel	25 Jan 1750/1		B	390-392
Dean, James	14 Nov 1776		CC	240-241
Dean, Mary			R(2)	439-440
Dean, Nathaniel	13 Nov 1767	Charles Town	X	239-240
Dean, Thomas	11 Apr 1752		R(1)	385
Dearington, Thos.			V	528-529
Deas, David	25 Sep 1775	Washaw, Santee	BB	234-239
Deas, John	26 Feb 1759		T	131
Deas, John	7 Mar 1759		T	136-137
Deas, John			T	236
de Beaufain, Hector Berenger	25 Oct 1766	Charles Town	W	359-361
Dechamps, Francis Sr.	22 Feb ----		Z	497-498
Deedery, Isaac	31 Mar 1774	St. Helena Parish	&	318-319
Dehay, John Andrew	26 Jan 1760		T	285-286
Delabere, George	11 May 1761		T	624
[Delafare, Lewis]	12 Jul 1774	Charles Town	&	422
DelaHoyd, Richard	26 Sep 1777	Charles town	CC	355-356
DeLancy, Peter			Z	116-122
Deleisseline, Magdalen	5 May 1759		T	184
Delessline, Peter	20 Mar 1758		S	350
Deliesseline, John	10 Nov 1768		X	400-401
Delgrass, Francis	16 Jan ----	Charles Town	MM	250-253
Delony, John	6 Jun 1753		R(3)	14

Name	Date	Location	Vol. & pages
Delph, Joseph	12 Nov 1753		R(2) 78
Dempsey, Edward	1 Oct 1772		& 140-141
Dempsey, Edward	19 Jun 1775	near Charles Town	& 562
Dempsey, Edward & Mary			S 382-383
Denenton, Richard	7 Jan 1777	Camden District	BB 27
Denley, James			S 364
Dennis, Ann			MM 278
Dennison, George	26 Feb 1750/1	Christ Church Parish	B 343-345
Denny, John	25 Sep 1753		R(2) 74-75
Denton, John	4 Aug 1767		X 99-101
De St. Julian, Benjamin			R(2) 534
De St. Julian, Henry	19 Jan 1769		Y 55-56
De St. Julien, Joseph	2 May 1747	Berkley Co.	MM 98-101
De St. Julien, Joseph	22 Aug 1747		MM 161-162
De St. Julien, Peter	4 Aug 1752	Berkley Co.	R(1) 521-523
DeSaussure, Henry	16 Mar 1762		V 186-189
da Sweancey, Samuel	4 Oct 1755		R(2) 367-368
Detheridge, Esham	4 Feb 1754	St. Peters Parish, Purrysburgh	R(2) 152
Devant, John	10 Jan 1769	Portroyal	X 427-428
Devant, John	8 Apr 1777		AA 219-221
Deveaux, Collo. Andrew	12 Apr 1770	Prince Williams Parish	Y 285-288
Deveaux, Andrew Sr.	20 Feb 1754	Berkly Co.	R(2) 130-133
D'Eveaux, Magdalen	11 May 1759		T 215-216
Dewar, Alexander			R(2) 340
Dewes, Bethel	7 Mar 1759		T 175-177
Dewick, Henry Senr(?)	28 Feb 1750/1		B 403-405
Dewitt, Charles		St. Mathews Parish	Y 280
Dewitt, John	7 Mar 1758		S 351-351
Dexter, John	27 Sep 1761		T 240-241
Deyoung, Barnard	18 Dec 1777	Charlestown	CC 247-248
D'harriette, Benjamin		Charles Town	R(2) 445-449
D'harriette, Mrs. Martha	29 May 1760		T 314-322
D'harriette, Mrs. Martha	25 Oct 1760		T 391
Dick, Cap. George	11 Nov 1773	Charles Town	Z 484
Dick, Dr. George	20 Apr 1749		B 198-201
Dick, Dr. Jas.			Y 346
Dick, John	1 Aug 1766	Craven Co.	X 58-59
Dick, William		Prince Fredericks Parish	V 223
Dickenson, David			& 62
Dickeson, Francis	3 Dec 1767		X 342
Dickey, Moses			X 350-350b
Didcotte, John	23 Feb 1760		T 284
Dill, Mrs. Elizabeth	5 Mar 1756		R(2) 430-433
Dillon, Hugh	18 Mar 1771	Charles Town	Z 89-92
Dills, Joseph	12 Feb 1745/6		MM 89-90
Dingle, Alexander	3 Feb 1759		T 137
Dingles, Alexr.	7 Apr 1770		Y 224
Diston, [Martha]	18 Jun 1752		R(1) 388-389
Diston, Mrs. Sarah	22 May 1749		B 99-100
Diston, Thos	10 May 1749		B 147
Ditmon, John	25 July 1776	Ashley Ferry	CC 18
Dixon, John	18 Feb 1761		T 501-504
Dixon, Thomas	15 Jun 1747		MM 123
Dixon, Thomas	20 Apr 1769		Y 46-47
Dixon, William	24 Dec 1751		R(1) 309-310
Dobbie, David			CC 381-382
Dobbin, Hugh	25 Mar [1772?]		& 85-86
Dodd, John	16 Aug 1770	Charles Town	Y 335-337
Dogett, Elizabeth	1 Jul 1756		R(2) 490
Dolback, John George	8 Jun 1753		R(2) 46
Donald, Moses	3 Dec 1770		Y 352
Donavan, John	21 May 1774		& 391-392
Donnom, Jacob	3 Mar 1746		MM 12-13
Donnom, Jacob	16 Nov 1770		Z 64
Donnom, James	6 Jun 1776		C 15-18
Donnom, Jonathan	15 Mar 1775		AA 77-78
Donnovon, John	$ Aug 1766		W 295

Name	Date	Location	Vol. & pages	
Donovan, Sarah	24 May 1773		&	259
Dooly, Patrick	27 Jul 1769		Y	89
Dopson, Isaac	25 Jun 1767		W	460-461
Dopson, Isaac	13 Dec 1769	Berkly Co.	Y	163-164
Dorcey, Mich'l			&	316
Dorch, Nathan	1 May 1777		BB	70
Dorman, Michael	8 Jan 1774		Z	441
Dorrill, Robert			CC	313-314
Dorrill, Robert Junr.			AA	255
Doughty, Thomas	8 Aug 1755	Charles Town	R(2)	354-355
Douglas, William	11 Jun 1747		MM	116
Douxsaint, Paul			BB	154-157
Dow, John	1 Mar 1773		Z	301
Downes, Richard Jr.	20 Aug 1773	Charlestown	Z	245-247
Downing, Frances	20 Jan 1756	St. Georges Parish	R(2)	398-399
Dowse, Gideon	24 Mar 1746/7		MM	84-85
Dowse, Hugh	11 Feb 1761		T	581-583
Doyal, Thomas	17 Oct 1760		T	428
Doyley, Daniel	18 Jul 1770		Y	294-297
Dozer, Leonard	20 Apr 1777	Cheraw District	BB	43
Dozier, Leonard	25 Feb 1777		BB	30-31
Drage, Rev. Theodorus Swaine	13 Mar 1775	Camden	AA	144
Drain, William	3 Aug 1767	Charlestown	X	222
Drake, John	17 Nov 1749		B	185-186
Drake, John	1750-1753		R(2)	127-129
Drake, Jonathan			R(2)	322-323
Drake, Jonathan	1 May 1770		Y	278-280
Drake, Mrs. Mary	4 Jun 1768		X	374
Drayton, Francis	15 May 1755	Charles Town	R(2)	276-277
Drayton, Hon. Thomas	24 Mar 1761		T	638-645
Drennan, David	1 Jun 1774		&	390
Drew, Mrs. Margaret	12 Apr 1763		V	533
Drew, Capt. Nathaniel	8 May 1751	Williamsburgh	B	454-455
Drew, Samuel	29 Apr 1763		V	533
Driggers, Mathew	26 Aug 1765		Y	26-27
Dring, Mr.	16 Jul 1756		R(2)	536-538
Droze, Daniel Senr	5 Apr 1781		BB	172-173
Dubois, John			CC	28-30
Dubois, Susannah	19 Dec 1757		S	272-274
Duboise, John	15 Jun 1750		B	294-295
Dubose, Daniel	24 Apr 1755	St. James Santee, Craven Co.	R(2)	340-341
Dubose, Esther	21 Apr 1764		W	106
Dubose, Isaac	17 May 1773		Z	359-363
Dubose, Jonothan			Z	129-131
Dubose, Joshua	21 Apr 1764		W	105-106
Dubourdieu, Joseph	28 Jun 1774		&	438-442
Ducatt, George			T	400-401
Duce, Richard	28 Aug 1754		R(2)	185
Duckatt, Robert	20 Sep 1746		MM	1
Duckner, David	2 Nov 1768	Charlestown	X	411-413
Duff, Mrs.	25 Jun 1747		MM	156
Duff, James	-- Aug 1746		MM	95-96
Duff, James		Christ Church Parish	R(2)	209
Dugard, Benjamin	11 May 1768		X	314-315
Dukes, Mrs. Joan	13 Mar 1772		&	19-20
Dumay, Jean	25 Aug 1767	St. James Santee	X	212
Dunbar, Dr. Robert			R(2)	436-437
Duncan, George	3 Apr 1761		T	583-584
Duncan, John	6 Jun 1751		R(1)	31-32
Dunkin, Samuel	13 Jul 1771		Z	137
Dunlap, Alexander	30 Jan 1762		T	471-472
Dunlap, John	12 May 1763		V	462
Dunlap, Robert	3 Aug 1774	St. Marks Parish	AA	1
Dunlop, Patrick	27 May 1767	Charleston	W	436
Dunmire, Albert	1 Jul 1746	Wadmalaw Island	MM	3
Dunn, Drury	3 Apr 1771		Y	444
Dunn, Henry	22 May 1771		Z	33

Name	Date	Location	Vol. & pages	
Dunn, John			&	316
Dunnam, Ebenezer Junr.	16 Nov 1766		W	349-350
Dunnings, James	12 Oct 1781		BB	254-255
Dunnovon, Elizabeth			W	304
Dunwoody, Wm	27 Feb 1753		R(2)	18-20
Dupont, Abraham	13 --- 1762		T	544-551
Dupont, Alexr.	8 May 1751	Prince Frederick Parish	R(1)	8-10
Dupont, John	24 Jan 1765		W	206-208
Dupre, Cornelius	20 Nov 1747	Berkley Co.	MM	210-211
Dupre, Mrs. Jean	12 Mar 1749/50	St. James, Goose Creek	B	230
Durand, Thos	4 & 7 Feb 1774		&	416-417
Durant, Robert	14 Oct 1766	George Town	W	336-337
Durffey, Hugh	15 Jun 1753		R(2)	14-16
Durousseau, Susanna	25 May 1749		B	133
Dutarque, Capt. John	15 Jan 1767		W	378-382
Dutarque, Joseph	19 Sep 1751		R(1)	88-91
Dutarque, Lewis	10 Jan 1748/9		B	28-29
Dutarque, Mrs. Mary	24 Nov 1767		X	220-221
Duthie, James	26 Jan 1770		Y	281
Duthy, William	1 Nov 1752	Charles Town	R(1)	474-475
Duva, Mary			&	359-360
Duvall, Stephen	1780		BB	100-101
Dwight, Christiana	23 Jun 1764		W	126
Dwight, Rev. Daniel	4 Jul 1748		MM	337-345
Dwight, John	17 Feb 1770	All Saints Parish, Craven Co.	Y	198-200
Dymes, Robert	23 Feb 1760		T	294
Eagles, Martin	.7 Feb 1772		&	57-59
Easton, Christopher	10 Jun 1760		T	361-362
Eaton, Joshua	14 Oct 1765		X	45-46
Eaton, Samuel	28 Apr 1757	Edisto Island, Colleton Co.	S	120-123
Eberley, John	10 Jun 1767		W	464
Eberson, Thomas	12 Mar 1765		W	248-249
Eberson, William	19 Jul 1766		W	299-300
Eckhart, Christian	10 May 1773	Prince Williams Parish	&	245
Eddy, William			X	396-397
Eden, James	23 Jun 1762	St. Phillips Parish	V	237-238
Eden, Jonah			W	36-37
Edes, James	10 Apr 1758		S	383-385
Edes, Sarah	12 Mar 1767		W	393
Edgar, Samuel			R(1)	357-358
Edie, James			X	132-133
Edings, Abraham			B	270-271
Edings, Mrs. Theodora	23 Nov 1760		T	423
Edings, William	10 Apr 1756		R(2)	475-480
Edings, William	22 Apr 1767	Edisto Island	W	425-430
Edwards, Isaac	1 Jan 1753		R(2)	10
Edwards, John	19 Jan 1749/50		B	231-232
Edwards, John	1 Jun 1752		R(1)	387-388
Edwards, John	8 Nov 1770	St. Georges Parish	Y	337-341
Edwards, Joshua Jr.	9 Apr 1768	St. Marks Parish	X	343-344
Edwards, Thomas	4 Nov 1776	St. Davids Parish	AA	167
Edwards, Uriah	21 Jul 1776		W	310-312
Edwards, William	29 May 1758	Charles Town	S	385-386
Edwards, William	11 & 12 Jul 1775		AA	117-118
Edwards, William	Jan 1781		BB	130-132
Edwards, Wm.	21 Mar 1782		BB	254
Ehney, Eberhart	14 Oct 1767		X	216-217
Ehney, Ulrick	6 Jul 1764	Charles Town	W	233-234
Ehny, Christina	3 Sep 1777		AA	255-256
Ekells, Barbara	23 Feb 1778		CC	339
Ekells, Robert	26 Apr 1769		Y	66-67
Elbert, Hannah			Y	186
Elbert, William	12 Jun 1755		R(2)	353
Elder, William	13 Jul 1748		B	3-4
Elders, John	6 Jan 1772		&	3
Elders, John	13 Mar 1772	Berkley Co., Goose Creek	&	69
Elders, John	6 May 1771		Z	42

Name	Date	Location	Vol. & pages	
Elicott, John & Martha	1764		W	142
Ellerbee, Edward	23 Nov 1770	St. Davids Parish, Craven Co.	Y	361-363
Ellerbee, Thomas	29 Feb 1750/1		B	383-395
Ellicott, Joseph	29 Sep 1768		X	388
Elliot, Bernard	3 Jan 1759	Chas. Town	T	124-127
Elliot, Mrs. Sarah	2 Jan 1775	St. Andrews Parish	&	503-507
Elliot, Capt. Thomas Law	6 Apr 1757		S	71-75
Elliot, William	3 Nov 1767	Charles Town	X	305-313
Eliot, Wm son of John	25 Mar 1751		B	457
Elliott, Artimas	23 Jun 1761		T	632
Elliott, Elizabeth Bellinger	12 Apr 1755		R(2)	329
Elliott, Humphrey			R(2)	433
Elliott, Humphry	12 Sep 1755		R(2)	362-363
Elliott, Jehu	27 Mar 1762		V	180-184
Elliott, Joseph	19 Jan 1768		X	247-249
Elliott, Joseph	1768-1771		Y	463
Elliott, Mary	25 Mary 1751		B	457-458
Elliott, Stephn.	25 Mar 1751		B	444-445
Elliott, Thomas	28 Mar 1761	St. Pauls Parish	T	554-565
Elliott, Thomas	18 Jul 1768	St. Bartholomews Parish	X	358
Elliott, Thomas Senr	25 Jul 1761	St. Pauls Parish	T	566-568
Elliott, William	15 Aug 1777	Charles Town	AA	255
Ellis, Edmond	13 Feb 1775	PortRoyal Island	&	541-543
Ellis, John	15 Jan 1757		S	39
Ellis	16 Jun 1768		X	351-352
Ellis, Mrs. Judith	29 Oct 1772	Charles Town	&	183-184
Ellis, Mrs. Mary	22 Aug 1781		BB	201
Ellis, Thomas			T	267b
Ellis, William			W	331
Ellis, William	24 Feb 1773		&	213-217
Ellis, William	12 Nov 1774	Charles Town District	&	575-576
Ellis, William	23 Jul 1773		&	284-285
Ellison, Matthew	25 Jan 1769	Craven Co.	X	434
Ellison, Robert	4 Dec 1758		T	100
Ellison, Robert	11 Jul 1772	Craven Co.	&	139
Elmes, Anne	1756		R(2)	394
Elmes, Benjamin	25 Sep 1746		MM	37
Elmore, Mathias	18 Apr 1768		X	342-343
Elmore, William	18 Apr 1768		X	342-343
[Else?], Thomas	11 Sep 1776		CC	77-83
Elsmore, James	13 Oct 1767		X	213
Emmery, Isaac	19 Oct 1764		W	159
Emsden, Ambrose	14 May 1774	St. Helena Parish	&	346-347
Epley, Benjamin	15 Feb 1777	Orangeburgh District	AA	175-176
Erhard, Abraham	28 Oct 1758	Purrisburg, Granville Co.	T	76-78
Ernst, John	22 Oct 1781		BB	241
Ervin, James			CC	236
Ervin, John	20 Apr 1773	Williamsburgh	Z	358
Ervin, Robert	30 Apr 1777		BB	54
Esdale, John	8 Nov 1776		AA	154
Evance, Thos	14 Feb 1781		BB	108-109
Evans, Alexander	7 May 1767		W	461-462
Evans, Benjamin	22 Mar 1775	Great Lynches Creek, St. Davids Parish	&	551
Evans, Branfield			R(1)	500-502
Evans, Evan	22 Jan 1778		CC	330-332
Evans, Johanna Christian			T	241-243
Evans, John	11 May 1753	Craven Co.	R(2)	41-43
Evans, John	26 Feb 1770	St. Helena Parish, Granville Co.	Y	210-212
Evans, John	20 Dec 1774	St. Helena Island, Granville Co.	AA	62-67
Evans, Rev. John	26 Mar 1770		Y	267-270
Evans, Jonathan	-- Feb 1746/7		MM	87-89
Evans, Mary widow	21 Jan 1762	St. George Parish	V	107
Evans, Phillip	6 Mar 1754		R(2)	135-137
Evasn, Samuel	27 Nov 1755	James Island, Berkley Co.	R(2)	404-405

Name	Date	Location	Vol. & pages	
Evans, William	8 Mar 1781	Edisto Island	BB	153-154
Evans, William	24 Jul 1754		R(2)	120
Evans, William	26 Mar 1770		Y	242-243
Evans, William	6 Aug 1772		&	140
Eycott, John			R(1)	56-57
Eycott, John	7 Aug 1751		R(2)	173
Fabian, James	10 Sep 1768		X	385-387
Fabian, Jonathan	13 May 1776		CC	24-25
Fabian, Joseph	23 Jun 1773	St. Pauls Parish	&	274-276
Fabian, Jonathan	13 May 1776		CC	69-71
Fabian, Mrs. Mary	23 Jan 1750/1		B	380-381
Fabian, William	17 Feb 1772	Colleton Co.	&	27-28
Fagans, Thos.			Y	270
Fairchild, Mary Ann	7 Feb 1760		T	293
Fairchild, Robert	4 Dec 1775		CC	4-5
Fairweather, Robert	2 Jul 1763		V	489-492
Falkingham, Ann	23 Jul 1747		MM	202
Fardoe, Thos	12 Feb 1772	Chas Town	&	37-38
Farell, Daniel	2 Aug 1758		T	38-39
Farell, Joseph	16 Feb 1774		Z	556-557
Farmer, Rev. Richard	12 Feb 1770	St. Johns, Berkley Co.	Y	190-192
Farquharson, James	Mar 1781		BB	201
Farr, Thomas Snr.	27 Jan 1777		CC	155-159
Farrell, John	7 Oct 1776	St. Andrews Parish	BB	23
Farris, Jane	8 Dec 1777		CC	306
Farwell, Henry	19 Aug 1772	Prince Georges Parish, Craven Co.	&	141-142
Faucheraud, Charles	24 Jun 1766		W	306-308
Faucheraud, Gideon	10 Jan 1754		R(2)	95-98
Faucheraud, Gideon	1 Jul 1771	Charles Town	Y	459
Favell, Thomas	26 Feb 1746/7		MM	92-93
Feaureau, William		Hilton head	&	138-139
Featherstone, Richard	9 Oct 1776		AA	151-153
Felstead, Adam	8 Feb 1774		Z	527
Feltham, Joseph	27 Aug 1771		&	49
Femster, John	16 Mar 1761		T	536
Fendin, Abraham	14 Jan 1767		X	138-139
Fendin, John	5 Sep 1766		X	57-58
Fendin, John Senr	10 Apr 1759		T	268
Fendin, Martha	16 Feb 1767		W	370-371
Fenwicke, Edward	26 Sep 1775		&	625-632
Fenwicke, Jno. (a free Negroe)	18 Sep 1769		Y	119
Ferguson, Mrs. Catherine	31 Mar 1752		R(1)	325-326
Ferguson, Charles	13 Dec 1763		V	505-507
Ferguson, Daniel	17 Mar 1775	Black Mingo	AA	93-98
Ferguson, Hugh	25 Jan 1768	St. Bartholomews Parish	X	277-278
Ferguson, Mary widow	19 Aug [1773]		&	295
Ferguson, Robert	28 Dec 1773		Z	434
Ferguson, William	31 Dec 1751		R(1)	367-369
Ferguson, William	19 Aug 1773	Prince Williams Parish, Granville Co.	&	294-295
Ferguson, William	1 Nov 1770		Y	345-346
Ferrell, John	27 Dec 1773	St. Marks Parish	Z	442
Ferry, Major Champness	3 Jun 1777		AA	214
Fetters(?), Francis	25 Mar 1748		B	47
Fick, George	26 Dec 1766		W	353-354
Fickling, Jeremiah			W	233
Fidling, Jacob	6 Mar 1746/7		MM	101
Field, Charles	19 Apr 1754		R(2)	186
Field, James	7 May 1756	Colleton Co.	R(2)	455-456
Field, John		Colleton Co.	W	187-188
Field, John Waight	5 Mar 1767		W	436-437
Field, Richard	14 Mar 1763	Colleton Co.	V	380-383
Field, William	22 May 1767	Bartholomew's Parish, Colleton Co.	W	441-442
Fike, George	12 Feb 1767	Gerkley Co.	X	18-21

Name	Date	Location	Vol. & pages
Filbin, John	24 Apr 1747		MM 94-95
Filbin, John	27 Jan 1774		Z 533
Filly, Benjamin	9 Aug 1777		CC 356-357
Finch, Isabella widow	23 Sep 1761	Charles Town	V 48-49
Fincke, Dr. John Augustus	24 Jul 1772	Black Mingo	& 130-134
Findley, John	20 Dec 1762		V 344-345
Findley, John	27 Feb 1770		Y 207
Findly, John	3 Mar 1777		BB 27
Finley, Mrs. Sarah	27 Feb 1770		Y 208
Fishburn, Thomas	1 Apr 1767	Colleton Co.	W 389-390
Fishburn, William			S 31
Fishburn, William	2 Feb 1761		T 442-444
Fisher, Mrs.	26 Mar 1751		R(1) 67
Fisher, Mrs. Henrietta	13 Dec 1750		R(1) 32-33
Fisher, Prudence	1 Sep 1770		Y 312
Fiskes, William			R(1) 474
Fitch, Jonathan	9 Apr 1752		R(1) 333-334
Fittig, Nicholas	2 Aug 1774	St. Georges Parish	& 464-465
Fitzgerald, Dr. Alexander	1 Feb 1773		Z 354-356
Fitzgerald, Dr. Alexander			& 255-256
Fitzgerald, John	24 Nov 1767		X 216
Fitzgerald, Larey	22 Nov 1766		W 348
Fitzgerald, Luke			B 103
Fitzpatrick, William	7 Mar 1767		X 60
Flannagan, John	11 Apr 1777		BB 42
Fleet, James	26 Jul 1764		W 173-174
Fleming, Alexander	30 Jun 1761		V 20-21
Fleming, Elizabeth	13 Sep 1776		& 616
Fleming, John	6 Apr 1751	Williamsburgh	B 417
Fleming, John	11 Oct 1768	Prince Fredericks Parish, Craven Co.	X 395
Fleming, Maurice			X 377-378
Fleming, Sarah	26 Jan 1767		W 373-374
Fleming, Thomas	4 Dec 1751	Johns Island	R(1) 157-161
Fleming, Thomas	6 Feb 1758	Ashepoo	T 101-103
Fleming, William	23 Nov 1750		B 342-350
Fletcher, Benjamin			T 270
Fletcher, Samuel	16 Mar 1778		CC 414
Flew, William	17 July 1754		R(2) 251-252
Flin, William	4 Apr 1774		& 382-390
Flint, James	7 Apr 1747		MM 81-82
Flinthem, Edward	7 Apr 1769		X 445-446
Flinthem, Edward	28 Nov 1771		Z 163-165
Flinthem, Edward	2 Dec 1772	Berkley Co.	& 168
Flower, Joseph Edward	17 Feb 1757		S 104-110
Flower, Col. Jos Edward	3 Mar 1757	Beaufort	S 110-115
Flowers, John			BB 16
Flud, James	11 Jan 1766		W 290
Fogartie, David	22 Jan 1770		Y 197-198
Fogartie, Stephen	24 Mar 1757		S 43-44
Fogartie, Steven Junr.	11 Apr 1775		& 559
Foissin, Elias	29 & 30 Apr 1767		X 68-76
Folk, Jacob	4 Dec 1777	fork between Broad & Saludy	BB 72-73
Foord, Capt. Thos.	10 Jun 1767		X 94-97
Popell, Elizabeth	30 Sep 1767		X 172-173
Forbes, John Junr.	1 Jul 1766		W 305-306
Ford, George	13-17 Sep 177-	Prince George Parish	CC 96-99
Ford, Kezia	18 Feb 1774		Z 490
Ford, Mrs. Mary	12 Dec 1755		R(2) 406-407
Ford, Stephen	7 Jan 1757	Prince George Parish	S 16-17
Ford, Thomas	16 Jan 1753		R(1) 506-507
Ford, Thomas			W 352
Ford, Thomas		Catawba River, Craven Co.	X 184
Ford, Thomas	3 Jul 1773	St. Bartholomews Parish	Z 381-382
Ford, Thomas	26 Feb 1774		Z 498-499
Ford, William	1774		AA 30
Ford, William Richard	21 Jun 1768	Colleton Co.	X 421
Fordyce, Isaac	5 Nov 1773		Z 413-414

Name	Date	Location	Vol. & pages	
Fordyce, Revd. John	17 Jul 1751		R(1)	314-322
Foreau, Charles Williams	14 Sep 1768		X	402-403
Forrester, William	4 Mar 1774	Craven Co., Winyaw	Z	515
Forster, Dr. Thomas			Y	164-165
Forsyth, James	3 Dec 1774	Broad River, Ninety Six District	&	493-499
Fort, Arthur	15 Aug 1773		&	308-309
Fosquet, John	30 Dec 1762		V	340
Fotheringham, Dr. Alexander	11 Feb 1777		CC	167-170
Fothringham, Dr. Thos.	14 Nov 1752		R(2)	13
Foust, Caspar	19 Feb 1777		CC	162-164
Foust, Henry	18 Sep 1777		CC	382-383
Fowler, Benoney	25 Jan 1762		V	31-32
Fowler, Christopher	8 Oct 1750	George Town	B	354-355
Fowler, Christopher	13 Sep 1753	George Town, Winyaw	R(2)	51-52
Fowler, Edward	2 Oct 1751	Charles Town	R(1)	94-103
Fowler, Edward	12 Aug ----	Charles Town	R(1)	422-427
Fowler, Gilbert			V	193-194
Fowler, James	25 Sept 1753		R(2)	56-63
Fowler, James	19 Dec 1772	Chas Town	&	179-183
Fowler, Jonathan		Christ Church Parish	&	308
Fowler, Richard	22 Feb 1757		S	123-124
Fowler, Thomas	15 Jun 1769		X	467
Fox, Joseph			R(2)	467
Fraiser, Ann			R(2)	163
Frampton, John	30 Oct 1776	Prince William Parish	AA	155-156
Frampton, Jonathan	11 Aug 1763		V	501-504
Francis, Vincent	20 Feb 1747		BB	28
Fraser, John	20 Aug 1754	Charles Town	R(2)	163
Frazar, Isaac	7 Mar 1777		AA	185
Frazer, John	25 Nov 1772		Z	289-290
Frazer, Judith Junr.	31 May 1764	Charles Town	W	101
Frederick, John	2 Dec 1751		R(1)	163
Freeman, Benjamin	28 Nov 1763		V	507-508
Freeman, John	28 Jun 1763		V	487-488
Freeman, Joseph	14 Jul 1777	96 District	BB	70
Freeman, William	13 Dec 1774		&	501
Preer, Solomon	9 Sep 1781		BB	207-208
Freer, William	6 Apr 1753	Johns Island	R(2)	49-50
Frewin, William	4 Feb 1767	Charles Town	X	130-131
Friday free Negro	18 Sep 177		CC	231-232
Frier, Mrs. Judith	25 Apr 1772		&	99-101
Frierson, James	3 Mar 1778		CC	411
Frierson, John			V	4
Frierson, John Junr.	3 Feb 1775	Camedon District	&	531
Frierson, William Sr.	21 Dec 1773	Williamsburgh Township	Z	518
Prieston, George	19 Apr 1750		B	262
Frink, John	18 Aug 1761		V	34-36
Frinks, John	15 Jun 1771	Prince George Parish, Craven Co.	Z	17
Fripp, John	7 Nov 1781		BB	230-231
Frisell, Elizabeth	11 Feb 1760		T	464-465
Frisel, Mary	10 Mar 1771		Y	449
Frisel, William	7 Jan 1761		T	464
Frizel, Alexander	19 Mar 1750/1		B	443-444
Frogatt, Adin	18 Apr 1764		W	72
Fromant, George	5 Mar 1777		AA	184-185
[Frost, Mary]			X	147
Fry, Baynard	6 Oct 1757		S	221-224
Fry, Ichibord	25 Mar 1751		B	437
Fry, Jacob			&	610
Fryar, John	11 Jul 1758		S	438-439
Frydig, Martin	25 Oct 1758		T	89-90
Fryerson, Thos.	21 Jan 1771	Craven Co.	Y	393
Fulleker, Henry	3 Jun 1769	Charles Town	Y	48-49
Fuller, Benja.	12 Apr 1751		R(1)	16-20
Fuller, Benjamin			R(2)	503-504

Name	Date	Location	Vol. & pages	
Fuller, Elizabeth	26 Jan 1758		S	329-331
Fuller, Joseph	2 Jul 1756		R(2)	501-503
Fuller, Mrs. Mary			R(1)	84
Fuller, Nathaniel	10 Feb 1749/50		B	240-241
Fuller, Mrs. Sarah widow	20 Feb 1754	Charles Town	R(2)	120-122
Fuller, Whitmarsh	17 Mar 1770		Y	270-273
Fuller, William			T	49
Fuller, William	27 Oct 1766		W	332
Fulmer, Matthew	29 Oct 1759		T	266
Fulmer, Michael	25 Feb 1762		V	109
Fulton, David			X	63-66
Furguson, Elizabeth	10 Mar 1755		R(2)	315
Futhey, Francis	20 Jun 1753		R(2)	43
Futhy, Robt.	20 Jun 1753		R(2)	44-45
Futhy, Robert	21 Mar 1754	Black Mingo, Craven Co.	R(2)	400-401
Futhy, Saml	5 Nov 1771		&	11
Fysse, Doctor William	10 & 12 Mar 1772		&	54-57
Gadsden, Thos.	16 Mar 1770		Y	250-263
Gafford, John	15 Feb 1752	St. Thomas Parish	R(1)	328b-330
Gaillard, Bartholomew	13 Apr 1770		Y	243-244
Gaillard, Bartholomew	11 Jun 1773		&	266-267
Gaillard, David	6 Feb 1781	St. Stephens Parish	BB	105-107
Gaillard, James	23 Feb 1769	St. James Santee	X	435
Gale, Hannah	8 Sep 1739		B	22-23
Galivan, James	8 Sep 1775		&	522-523
Gallman, Henry	10 Mar 1768	Saxegotha Township	X	356-358
Gallman, Henry	13 Feb 1777	Congarees, Saxagotha Township	CC	194-196
Gallman, John	21 Jul 1758		T	22-23
Gamble, Edward	26 Jan 1762		V	90
Ganaway, John	1 Sep 1758		T	53
Garden, Rev. Alexander Senr.	15-19 Oct 1756	Charles Town	S	91
Garden, Dr. Francis			Y	397-398
Garden, Simon	4 Jan 1775		AA	56
Gardner, Daniel			R(1)	141-142
Gardner, Geo:	11 Jan 1763		V	320-322
Gardner, Melchor	25 Nov 1765	St. Pauls Parish	X	195-197
Gardner, William	11 Jun 1751		R(1)	28-29
Gardner, William		Williamsburgh	W	316
Garnes, Capt. William	20 Nov 1762		V	299-300
Garrardeau, James	4 May 1776		CC	7-9
Garret, James	21 Jul 1769		Y	123
Garvey, John	Jan 1758		T	93
Garveny, John	6 Jun 1768	St. Lukes Parish	X	364
Gasque, John	1 Aug 1777		CC	230-231
Gaultier, Dr. Joseph	3 Sep 1746		MM	16-22
Gaultier, Mary	22 Oct 1750		B	340-342
Gegar, John Conrad	6 May 1773		&	305-307
Geigelman, Ralph	24 Mar 1772		&	45-46
Geiger, Jacob	4 Aug 1761		V	33-34
Geiger, Jacob Jr.	23 Nov 1772	Berkley Co.	Z	414-415
Geiger, Michael	13 Jan 1768	Berkley Co., St. Georges Parish	X	322
Geiger, Herman			R(1)	107-109
Geigleman, Emanuel	15 Mar 1773	St. Bartholomew Parish	&	218-219
Gelzer, Daniel	22 Apr 1757		S	101-103
Gelzer, Daniel	8 May 1760		T	305
Gelzer, Daniel	12 Jan 1761		T	427
Gelzer, Daniel	20 Jan 1761		T	454
Gelzer, Daniel	5 Dec 1780		BB	128
Gendron, John Jr.	7 Jan 1756	St. James Santee	R(2)	395-397
Gerald, James	13 Dec 1760		T	439
Gerrald, Mrs. Mildred	19 Aug 1766		W	324-325
Gerrardeau, John	8 Dec 1747		MM	214-216
Geygar, George Frederick	29 Jan ----		B	380
Gib, Dr. Robert	31 Jan 1778	Peedee	CC	415-419

Name	Date	Location	Vol. & pages	
Giball, Knight	3 Oct 1774	Charles town	&	443-444
Gibbes, Mrs. Ann	16 May 1771	John's Island	&	26-27
Gibbes, Howell	25 Sept 1773		Z	397
Gibbes, John	21 Feb 1771		Y	432-434
Gibbes, Robert	19 Jun 1752		R(1)	408-409
Gibbons, John	14 Fev 1761		T	505
Gibbons, Joseph	2 Mar 1752	Wadmelaw Island	R(1)	352-353
Gibbons, Michael	30 Jan 1754		R(2)	169
Gibbs, John Sr.	9 Apr 1765		W	267-268
Gibbs, Peter	9 Mar 1773		&	209-210
Gibson, Alexander	26 Jan 1765	Charles Town	W	234
Gibson, Gideon	28 Sep 1776		AA	249-250
Gibson, Gilbert	26 Feb 1761		T	588-589
Gibson, Isham			X	396
Gibson, John	3 Feb 177-		AA	213-214
Gibson, Jothan		Christ Church Parish	Z	138
Gibson, Robert	1 Mar 1774	St. Mark's Parish	&	318
Gibson, Samuel	4 Dec 1771	Wateree River	Z	151-152
Gibson, William	15 Feb 1747/8	Charles Town	MM	254
Giger, Michael		St. Georges Parish	X	230-231
Gignilliatt, John	6 Jul 1750	Berkly Co.	B	287-288
Gilbert, Rev. John Lewis	21 Dec 1773		Z	511-515
[Giles, Abraham]	29 Apr 1771		Z	38-39
Gillespie, James	19 & 20 Jun 1755	Craven Co.	R(2)	355-356
Gillespie, John	12 Jul 1774		AA	10-12
Gilmor, James	19 Aug 1772		Z	250-252
Gilzer, John	17 Nov 1774		&	466-468
Gindra, Abraham	17 Jul 1767		X	161
Girardeau, James			S	41-43
Girardeau, Peter	13 Jan 1757	St. Bartholomews Parish	S	264-267
Girardin, Henry		Purysboro	R(2)	316
Gittens, John	9 Dec 1749		B	196
Given, Philip	31 May 1754	Granvill Co., Port Royal	R(2)	219-220
Glasco, Robert		Craven Co., Prince Frederick [Parish]	Z	434-435
Glass, Robert	20 Aug 1754		R(2)	235-236
Glass, Robert	3 Jul 1765	St. Pauls Parish	W	268-269
Glaze, Capt. James	18 Mar 1769		X	454-456
Glaze, John	24 Jun 1752		R(1)	397-398
Glaze, Matachi	19 May 1762		V	199-200
Glaze, Mrs. Sarah	2 Sep 1748		B	19-21
Glaze, William	25 Oct 1764		W	180-181
Glen, Daniel	29 Apr 1758		S	362-363
Glen, John Junr	27 May 1777		AA	237-238
Glen, John Senr	27 May 1777		CC	199-201
Glover, Charles Worth	6 May 1747		MM	97-98
Glover, George	12 Nov 1772		&	198-199
Glover, George	1774		AA	28
[Glover, Hannah]			W	192
Glover, John	18 Feb 1761		T	465-466
Glover, Susana	23 Jan 1767		X	144
Glover, William	29 Mar 1769		Y	104-106
Goddard, Francis	19 Dec 1777		CC	296-300
Goddard, Mary	25 Feb 1755	Charles Town	R(2)	325
Goddard, William	31 Jan 1759		T	128
Godeno, Mary	25 Apr 1752		R(1)	385
Godfrey, Rd.	16 Jun 1747		MM	132
Godfrey, Robert	21 May 1759		T	191
Godfrey, Robert	20 Apr 1761		T	179-180
Godfrey, Thomas	5 Apr 1762	St. Andrews	V	144-145
Godfrey, Thos.	30 Aug 1776		C	73-77
Godfrey, William	13 Oct 1770		Y	343
Godin, Benjamin	20 & 21 Jun 1749	Goose Creek	B	107-123
Godin, David	28 Jul 1755	Ashepoo	R(2)	357-360
Godin, Isaac	22 Jan 1778		CC	320-326
Godin, Mrs. Marriane	10 Sept 1755		R(2)	363-364
Godwyn, Jesse			Y	5-8
Golightly, Culcheth	31 Mar 1753		R(1)	534-546

Name	Date	Location	Vol. & pages	
Golightly, Culcheth	16 Jan 1748		B	244-246
Golightly, Culcheth	16 Apr 1751	St. Bartholomews Parish, Colleton Co.	B	436-437
Golightly, Culcheth	7 Jul 1763	Charles Town	V	446-457
Good, Dr. John	4 Apr 1748		MM	322-323
Goodbee, Alexander	18 Jun 1752		R(1)	401
Goodbee, Hanh.	29 Jul 1762		V	243-244
Goodwin, Elizabeth	10 May 1749		B	100
Gordon, Alexander	Oct 1755		R(2)	270-271
Gordon, Alexander	2 Jan 1762		V	118-122
Gordon, Benjamin	15 Oct ----		V	242-243
Gordon, Charles	25 May 1776		&	601-603
Gordon, Charles	25 May 1776		CC	19-21
Gordon, Rev. Charles	7 Apr 1768		X	283
Gordon, James	2 Jan 1764	Black Mingo	W	19
Gordon, James	4 May 1771	Charles Town	Y	453-456
Gordon, John	3 May 1757	Berkley Co.	S	143-144
Gordon, Mary	10 Jul 1766	Craven Co., Williamsburg	W	309
Gordon, Roger	27 Aug 1751		R(1)	92
Gordon, Thomas	15 May 1766		W	296-297
Gossling, George	8 Nov 1780	Charles Town	BB	208-212
Goudin, Theodore	18 & 19 Feb 1774	Prince Fredericks Parish	Z	521-527
Gough, Edward	31 Jul 1752		R(1)	435
Gough, John	26 Apr 1748		R(1)	170-172
Gough, Oneal	1 Jan 1752		R(1)	172-173
Gough, Oneal	20 Feb 1755		R(2)	308-309
Gough, Richard	8 Oct 1753		R(2)	81-84
Gould, William	28 Jan 1769		X	420-421
Goulding, Peter	1 Apr 1760		T	292-293
Gourdin, Lewis	14 May 1755		R(2)	333
Gourdin, Peter	8 Mar 1775	St. John's Parish	&	534-538
Gourdin, William	16 Feb 1761		T	493
Govan, Andrew	13 Feb 1772		&	12-14
Govan, John	27 Feb 1768	Charles Town	X	269-270
Gowdy, Robt	13 Nov 1776	Ninety Six [District]	AA	195-208
Gracia, Anthony			R(2)	368-369
Gracia, Francis	22 Jun 1764		W	120-121
Gradick, Richard	30 Jun 1773		&	293-294
Graham, Edward	13 Apr 1768		X	283
Graham, James			V	195-196
Grame, Wm	28 Nov 1772	Union St., Charlestown	&	184
Grange, Hugh	25 Apr 1747	Pon pon	MM	127-131
Grange, Hugh			V	196-198
Grange, Jane	30 Jan 1756		R(2)	405
Graves, Mrs. Agnes	6 Feb 1768		X	250
Graves, Charles	19 Apr 1769		Y	51-52
Graves, Charles	9 Sep 1776		&	611-612
Graves, Charles	9 Sep 1776		CC	36-37
Graves, Eliza.	9 Sep 1776		&	610-611
Graves, Eliza.	9 Sep 1776		CC	35-36
Graves, James	25 Apr 1771		Y	444-445
Graves, John	9 Aug 1771	Prince Williams Parish	Z	48-53
Graves, Leonard	26 Aug 1767		Y	10-11
Graves, Thomas			W	186-187
Graves, Wm.	10 Jun 1755		R(2)	342
Gray, George	17 Mar 1778		CC	401-402
Gray, Robert	10 Jan 1778		CC	337
Grayson, John	26-28 Jan ----		CC	342-344
Greaves, Alexander	13 Mar 1762		V	114
Green, Benjamin	8 Apr 1768	Hilton Head, Granville Co.	X	291-294
Green, Elizabeth			W	391-392
Green, Isaac	25 Jul 1772	St. Marks Parish	Z	228-229
Green, John	14 Mar 1750/1		R(1)	26-28
Green, Rev. John		Granville Co., St. Helena Parish	X	83-85
Green, Peter	15 Jan 1768		X	245-246
Green, Robert	15 May 1773		Z	364
Green, Mrs. Sarah	1 May 1777		BB	228

Name	Date	Location	Vol. & pages
Green, Samuel	23 Oct 1770		Y 346-349
Greene, Doctor John	8 Dec 1772	Prince Williams Parish, Granville Co.	& 175-176
Greening, Mason	28 Dec 1776		BB 15
Greenland, Ann	28 Feb 1778	St. Stephens	CC 395
Greenland, Mrs. Cath.	26 Dec 1761		V 112-113
Greenland, John			CC 183
Greenswood, Francis	2 Apr 1771	Charles Town	Z 40
Gregg, Leonard	30 Mar 1775		& 553
Gregory, Benjamin Senr	25 Sep 1761		V 50
Greham, Arthur	20 Mar 1777		BB 33
Grenier, Andrew	7 Jan 1752		R(1) 164
Grennan, Capt. John	21 Sep 1764		W 176
Greville, Doctor Samuel			& 513
Grier, Andrew	6 Nov 1766		W 362
Grier, Andrew	10 Apr 1773	Prince George's Parish	& 301-302
Grier, Joseph	26 Sept 1768		X 395-396
Grier, Patrick	11 Oct 1768	Prince Georges Parish	X 392-394
Grier, Samuel	25 May 1772		Z 223-224
Grier, William	5 Jul 1768		X 355
Griffin, Joyce widow	16 Oct 1749		B 173
Grimbal, Thos			S 351
Grimball, Charles	11 Jul 1770	St. Michaels Parish, Charles Town	Y 292-293
Grimball, Hannah	11 Feb 1771	Edisto Island	Y 447-449
Grimball, Isaac	8 Dec 1752	Charles Town neck, St. Philips Parish	R(1) 476-477
Grimball, Joshua	13 Jan 1758		S 333-341
Grimball, Joshua	14 Apr 1768	Edisto Island	X 344-345
Grimball, Joseph	23 Oct 1777		CC 377-378
Grimball, Paul	14 Feb 1750/1	St. Helena Island	B 429-433
Grimball, Paul	9 Feb 1757	Edisto Island	S 60-61
Grimball, Paul			W 456-457
Grimbol, Rebeckah	5 Jun 1767	Granvill Co., St. Helena Parish	X 66-68
Grimes, William	7 Feb 1749/50		B 225
Grimes, Wm.	11 May 1770		Y 238-239
Grindley, James	6 Aug 1765	Charles Town	W 278-286
Grive, Alexander	27 Oct 1770		Y 343
Grive, Joseph	1 Jun 1774		X 393-395
Groom, Thomas	1 Nov 1766		W 339-340
Groomes, Thomas	12 Sep 1763		V 500
Grove, Samuel	22 Mar 1781	Beaufort	BB 173
Grove, Samuel	15 Jul 1776	Beaufort	CC 12-14
Grunland, Will:	10 May 1762		V 206-207
Grunsweig, Frederick	14 Jan 1765	Charles Town	W 208-210
Guearin, Peter	18 Mar 1774		Z 530
Guerard, John (Hon.)	30 May 1764	Berkley Co.	W 109-117
Guerin, Henry	13 Apr 1772	St. Thomas & St. Denis Parish	& 103-109
Guerrin, Isaac	17 Jan 1758		S 274-280
[Guerin, John]	1 Jan 1757		S 14-15
Guerin, Mrs. Martha Esther	11 May 1781	St. Thomas Parish, Berkly Co.	BB 174
Guerin, Mary	17 Nov 1777		CC 354-355
Guerin, Mary Johnston			AA 246
Guerin, Mathurin	7 Apr 1781	St. Andrews Parish	BB 229-230
Guerin, Robert			AA 246
Guerin, Robt			CC 18-19
Guerry, Stephen		St. James Santee, Craven Co.	& 113-115
Guiger, [Jacob]	25 Oct 1769		Y 155-157
Guinard, Gabriel	7 Oct 1757		S 191-193
Guiness, John	16 Oct 1777		CC 279
Gunn, William			V 225-226
Gunter, Edward	21 Oct 1776		CC 112-122
Guy, Rev. William	29 Jan 1750/1	Ashley River	B 365-368
Gwyn, Maurice	24 Jun 1749	Charles Town	B 124

Name	Date	Location	Vol. & pages
Hacket, Mrs. Elizabeth	25 Aug 1769		Y 135-137
Haddrell, Susanah	20 Jan 1761		T 467-468
Haggard, John		Ninety Six District	CC 286-287
Hahnbaum, Benjamin			Z 486-487
Haig, George	30 Oct 1749	Congrees	B 174-176
Hails, George			& 552
Hails, Thomas	15 Jan 1762		V 87-88
Hains, Nicholas	15 Feb 1747/8	Charles Town	MM 253
Hakins, Masters			W 1
Hales, Alaner	4 Oct 1777		CC 392
Hales, William	3 Jul 1781		BB 227-228
Haley, James	10 Apr 1762		V 185
Hall, Dr. Benjamin	16 Oct 1750		B 384-385
Hall, George	8 Aug 1754	Berkley Co.	R(2) 261-262
Hall, John Jr.	26 Aug 1772		Z 253-254
Hall, [Thomas]	8 Feb 1757		S 49-51
Hall, Thomas Sr.	9 May 1768		X 363
Hall, William	28 Apr 1768		Y 106-111
Halloway, Richard	19 Jan 1762		V 85
Hallum, Basil	14 Dec 1772	St. Pauls Parish	& 177
Haly, Doctor John	15 Oct 1776		AA 168-171
Ham, John	22 Mar 1774	St. Davids Parish	& 336-337
Hambelton, Archibald			MM 328-329
Hamilton, Archibald	19 Feb 1767		X 61-63
Hamblin, Geo.	28 Aug 1746		MM 1-3
Hamilton, George			R(2) 217-218
Hamilton, George	27 Apr 1762		T 541
Hamilton, Hector	8 Mar 1747/8		MM 278
Hamilton, James			B 52-53
Hamilton, James			W 10
Hamilton, John		St. Johns Parish	V 80-81
Hamilton, John	31 Dec 1774	WilliamsBurgh Township, Craven Co.	& 511
Hamilton, Pringle			T 530-531
Hamilton, Robert	31 Jul 1755		R(2) 366-367
Hamilton, Rosannah			AA 61-62
Hamilton, Stephen	31 Mar 1750		B 252-254
Hamilton, William	7 Aug 1777		CC 238-239
Hamlin, George	3 Feb 1746/7		MM 71
Hamlin, Samuel	21 Nov 1775		CC 61-62
Hamlin, Thomas Senr.	28 Apr 1767		W 435
Hampton, Mrs. Ann	12 Jun 1777	Charles Town District	AA 232-233
Hampton, John			T 360
Hampton, Preston	2 Jul 1751		R(1) 109-110
Hampton, Preston	20 Sep 1777	Ninety Six District	CC 338
Hampton, William			X 141-142
Hanahan, John	26 Jul 1763	Edisto Island	V 547
Handcock, Elizabeth	20 Mar 1752	Charles Town	R(1) 324-325
Handcock, Mary			T 203
Handcock, Robert			R(2) 414
Handlen, Champernow	29 Oct 1760		T 415
Handlen, Edward	12 Mar 1746/7		MM 198-200
Handlen, John	8 May 1754		R(2) 179-180
Handlen, John	-- Sept 1777		CC 376
Handlen, Thomas	1764		W 121
Handlin, Thomas	4 Mar 1750/1		B 426
Hanscome, Moses	30 Jan 1772		Z 202-203
Hanson, Micaljah	7 Aug 1777		CC 357
Harberd, James	22 Jan ----		Z 165-167
Hardcasll, Doctor Wm.			AA 254-255
Hardcastle, Henry			S 37
[Harden, Thomas]			R(1) 410-411
Harden, William	13 Jan 1761		T 433-434
Hardman(?), Volintine	6 Feb 1756		R(2) 414-415
Hardy, George		Charles Town	R(2) 1-2
Hardy, Matthew	2 Dec 1769	St. John Parish	Y 168-169
Hardy, Robt.	20 Jan 1762		V 126-129
Harfort, Jas. Senr.	10 Sept 1763		W 3

Name	Date	Location	Vol. & pages	
Harleston, Mrs. Elizabeth		14 Feb 1757	S	30-31
Harleston, John Junr.	8 Apr 1771		Y	428
Harleston, John Senr	14 Jul 1768		X	383-385
Harleston, Nocholas	29 Mar 1768	St. Johns Parish, Berkley	X	333-336
Harper, William	28 Apr 1761		T	615
Harrington, Whitmell	30 Oct 1746		MM	55-56
Harris, William	27 Apr 1752	Craven Co.	R(1)	370-372
Harris, Wm.			R(2)	535-536
Harris, Wm	8 Mar 1774	St. Hellena Parish	Z	515-516
Harrison, Christopher	14 Oct 1777		CC	335
Harrison, Margaret	18 Apr 1770		Y	225
Harrison, Thomas	18 Feb 1756		R(2)	424-426
Harrison, Thomas	15 Sep 1765		W	287
Harrison, William	14 Jul 1774		&	417
Harriss, Sarah	5 Oct 1751		R(1)	84
Harry, David			T	382-383
Harry, David	7 Nov 1773	St. Davids Parish	Z	478
Harry, Evan	28 Apr 1761		T	615
Harry, Jonathan			V	158
Hart, Arthur	30 Aug 1777		CC	249-253
Hart, Benjamin			Z	125-126[4pp]
Hart, Richard			Z	540-541
Hart, Robert minor	22 Jul 1773		&	295
Hart, William	27 Jun 1766		X	56-57
Hart, Wm.	30 Dec 1771	St. Georges Parish	Z	200-202
Hartee, Elijah	11 Sep 1769		Y	-18-119
Hartley, Henry	6 May 1768	Sax Gotha Township	X	313-314
Hartley, James	9 Jul 1759	St. Pauls Parish	T	218-222
Hartley, James	25 May 1761		V	160-175
Hartley, James	25 May 1765	Charles Town	W	286-287
Hartley, James	19 Apr 1773	St. Pauls Parish	&	257-258
Hartley, Thomas			Z	353-354
Hartley, Thomas	19 Apr 1773	Berkley Co.	&	258-259
Hartley, Thomas		Stono	&	556-557
Hartman, John			B	91-92
Hartman, Ruth widow	10 Mar 1767		W	393-394
Hartman, Mrs. Sarah	19 Jun 1774		&	423
Hartman, William	15 Jun 1747		B	25
Harty, David	31 Aug 1748	Prince George Parish	B	21
Harvey, Arnold	17 Oct 1764		W	144-147
Harvey, Benjamin	5 Jun 1756		R(2)	508-511
Harvey, Benjamin	7 Oct 1762		V	278-279
Harvey, Childers	16 Mar 1769		X	443
Harvey, Elizabeth			BB	48-49
Harvey, Hazzard	28 Jun 1775	• Beaufort, St. Helena Parish	CC	49-51
Harvey, Maurice		St. Georges, Dorchester	W	292-295
[Harvey,] Robert	28 Feb 1777	Charles Town	AA	211-212
Harvey, Samuel	3 Jun 1762		V	239
Harvey, William	19 Jan 1768	Beaufort, Port Royal	X	268-269
Hasel, Andrew	5 Mar 1764		W	26-27
Hasfort, Joseph	31 Oct 1769	St. Marks Parish	Y	185-186
Haskins, Benoni Peter	30 Jul 1771		Z	87-89
Haskins, Peter	11 Mar 1767		W	365-366
Hassel, John	22 Dec 1753		R(1)	517-521
Hasell, Thomas	23 Sept 1756	George Town	R(2)	543-555
Hasting, Archibald	9 May 1753	Granvill Co.	R(2)	31-32
Hatcher, James	22 May 1777		BB	65-66
Hatcher, Mr. Margret	4 Aug 1766		S	303
Hatley, Roger Peter Handasyde			Z	312
Hawkins, Edward	6 Jan 1775		&	538-539
Hawkins, John	15 Sep 1756	Fort moore, New Windsor	S	175-176
Hawkins, Robt	2 Dec 1776	Camden Dist.	CC	132
Hawkins, Robt	11 Dec 1776		CC	131
Hay, John	13 Apr 1772		&	48-49
Hay, John	30 Apr 1777		BB	54
Hay, Peter	22 May 1771	Congarees	Z	25-26
Hay, Susannah	13 Apr 1772		&	47-48
Haydon, John	10 Jun 1755		R(2)	342-343

Name	Date	Location	Vol. & pages	
Hayes, Cornelius		Amelia Township	W	363
Hayes, John			T	409-410
Hayne, Isaac	17 Mar 1752	St. Bartholomews Parish	R(1)	331-333
Hayne, William	29 Apr 1765		W	262-264
Haynsworth, John	5 Jun 1771		Y	459
Haynsworth, Richard	22 Apr 1762	Craven Co., St. Marks Parish	V	192
Hays, Mrs. Hannah	4 Jul 1749		B	131
Hazard, Col. William	12 & 13 Apr 1757		T	46-47
Hazelwood, Hannah	5 May 1764	George Town	W	138-139
Hazlewood, Edward	16 Jan 1761		T	495
Heap, Jonathan	15 Jun 1767		W	443
Heape, Benja.	17 Mar 1748/9		B	92-94
Heape, Harry	7 Apr 1749		B	129
Heape, Joseph	17 Apr 1749		B	130
Heape, Mary Ann	3 Oct 1777		AA	263
Heard, John Junr	6 Sep 1777		CC	333-334
Hearne, Elizabeth	17 Mar 1752		R(1)	389-391
Hearne, Peter			B	160-161
Hearly, Stephen	12 Jun 1759		T	252-253
Heichler, Nicholas	5 Aug 1777		CC	230
Heinlein, Mathias	13 Oct 1780		BB	85
Henderson, David	5 Oct 1771	Charles Town	Z	145-146
Henderson, James		Charles Town	&	249
Henderson, Reverend James	23 Dec 1780	Edisto	BB	97-98
Henderson, John	1 Apr 1751		B	419
Henderson, Peirce Robert		Charles Town	S	33-35
Hendrick, James	5 Nov 1757		S	208-209
Hendrick, Moses	23 Jan 1761		T	468-469
Hendrick, William	3 Mar 1749/50		B	235-236
Hendrie, Andrew	25 Jun 1760		W	318
Hennings, Mrs. Grace	11 Aug 1774		AA	19a; 6
Henry, Archibald	4 Feb 1760		T	286
Henry, Margaret Jean	24 Aug 1773		&	309
Hergrove, Joseph	24 Oct 1777		CC	365
Herman, Peter	16 Jun 1750	Berkley Co.	B	278-279
Heringdine, Silas	4 Aug 1770		Y	318
[Herring, John]	4 Jun 1765		W	267
Heskett, John			BB	132-133
Heskett, Joseph			B	438
Heskett, George			MM	228-237
[Hewitt], Dr. William			V	365-367
Hext, Alexander	4 Feb 1771	Ponpon, St. Bartholomews Parish, Colleton Co.	Y	382-384
Hext, Benjamin	19 Apr 1749		B	412-416
Hext, David	4 Mar 1755	Charles Town	R(2)	292-296
Hext, David			T	244-246
Hext, David	26 May 1772	St. Johns Parish, Colleton County	&	74-75
Hext, David	11 Feb 1768		X	282-283
Hext, Edward	31 May 1768		X	331
Hext, Edward			&	14-15
Hext, Francis	26 Sep 1746		MM	30-33
Hext, Joseph & Elizabeth			B	416
Hext, Joseph	14 Oct 1755		R(2)	367
Hext, Philip	7 May 1768	St. Bartholomews Parish	X	302-303
Hext, Sarah	2 Jun 1755		R(2)	335
Hext, Thos	14 Mar 1748/9		B	94-96
Hext, Thomas	24 Jun 1766	Wadmalaw Island	X	55-56
Hext, William	10 May 1754		R(2)	180-181
[Hext, Wm]			Z	14
Hext, [William]	17 May 1771	Prince Williams Parish	X	15-16
Heyer, Michael	9 May 1772		&	53-54
Heyler, Michael	30 Mar 1773	Saludy River	Z	423-425
Heyward, Daniel Junr.	7 Nov 1782		BB	262-263
[Heyward?, James]	25 May [1762?]		V	229-230
Heyward, John	7-8 Apr 1773		&	261-264
Heyward, Samuel	19 Nov 1766		W	344-345
Heywood, Revd. Henry		St. Phillips Parish	R(2)	394-395

Name	Date	Location	Vol. & pages	
Hiatt, Robert	16 May 1771		Z	14
Hicks, Geo.	6 Aug 1762	Craven Co.	V	249-250
Hicks, George	22 Oct 1765		W	288
Hiett, Anthony	4 Aug 1767		X	97-98
Hiett, Robert	25 May 1750		B	279-280
Higgins, George	19 Jun 1769		X	463
Hilburn, Thomas	27 Apr 1765		W	253-254
Hill, Charles	27 Jan 1752		R(1)	295-297
Hill, George			&	419-420
Hill, John	30 Apr 1748		B	11-12
Hill, John	14 Sep 1754	Berkley Co.	R(2)	253
Hill, John	3 Apr 1769	Charlestown	X	467-468
Hill, John	25 Sep 1777	St. Davids Parish	CC	241-242
Hill, Jonathan	22 Dec 1772		Z	293-294
Hill, Littleton			R(1)	303-306
Hill, Richard	25 Apr 1747		MM	302-303
Hill, Robt	1746	St. Bartholomews	B	1
Hill, Robert	4 Apr 1758		S	368-370
Hill, Robert	6 Mar 1759		T	152-159
Hill, Samuel	17 May 1770		Y	314-317
Hilsford, Joseph	15 Mar 1748/9	Goosecreek	B	338-339
Hinckley, William	25 Aug 1780	Charles Town	BB	133-134
Hircom, Christopher	11 Jun 1772	Prince Georges Parish, Waccamaw	&	91
[Hirn, Adam]	2 Sep 1774		&	509
Hitchins, Thomas	29 Aug 1749		B	170-171
Hodges, Henry	3 Jul 1758		T	26-27
Hodge, Thos.	3 Jul 1769	St. Andrews Parish	X	466
Hodsden, John	6 Sep 1776	Charles Town	&	606-608
Hodsden, John	6 Sep 1776	Charles Town	CC	30-33
Hodson, Thomas	16 Aug 1758		T	40-41
Hoff, Frederick	18 May 1774	Oringeburgh Township	&	399-400
[Hog], Richard	4 Jul 1769		Y	111-112
Hogg, George	28 Oct 1767		X	209-210
Hogg, George	23 Dec 1771		Z	150-151
Hogg, James	16 May 1774		&	352-355
Hogg, John			T	217-218
Hogg, John Junr.	18 Jun 1771		Z	24
Hogg, John Senr.	6 Feb 1771		Y	414-415
Hohn, Mrs. Catherine	12 Apr 1773		X	532
Holder, Mary	23 Aug 1777	Peedee	CC	236
Holiday, William	11 Aug 1781	Charlestown	BB	224-226
Holland, Daniel			R(2)	221-222
Holland, Dennis			BB	240-241
Holland, Joseph	24 Apr 1773		Z	340
Hollibush, John	6 Jul 1750		B	309-310
Hollingsworth, Abraham	27 Apr 1772		&	124-126
Hollingsworth, Samuel	8 May 1754	Craven Co.	R(2)	266-268
Hollingsworth, Samuel	10 Oct 1771	Craven Co., St. Davids Parish	Z	116
Hollybush, John & Sarah	21 Oct 1765		Y	31-32
Holman, Conrad	13 Jun 1772		&	89-91
Holman, Thomas	2 Apr 1756	St. Andrews Parish	R(2)	471-472
Holman, Thomas	21 Jan 1774	St. Andrews Parish	&	380-381
Holman, William	27 Apr 1756	St. Bartholomews Parish, Colleton Co.	R(2)	472-473
[Holmes, Elizth.]	5 Jan 1773		Z	291
Holmes, Mrs. Elizabeth	20 Apr 1773		&	267-268
Holmes, George	23 Oct 1753		R(2)	64
Holmes, Isaac	18 Feb 1752		R(1)	358-364
Holmes, Isaac		Charles Town	T	251-252
Holmes, Isaac			W	72-88
Holmes, Ralph	15 Nov 1749		B	385
Holmes, Solomon	1 Dec 1773		Z	450-451
Holmes, William		Jas Island	BB	140
Holms, Thomas	13 Dec 1776		BB	27
Holzendorf, Ernest	16 Mar 1762		V	189-190
Holzendorf, Rosina	13 Apr 1762		V	157-158
Holzendorf, Rosanna			V	53

Name	Date	Location	Vol. & pages	
Hood, Catherine	28 Mar 1771		Y	422
Hood, Jonathan	14 Sep 1773		Z	478
Hooffs, Hans Ernst	25 Oct 1765		X	43-45
Hook, Michael	19 Sep 1771	Broad River	Z	131-132
Hook, Peter	3 Sep 1758	Orangeburgh	T	166-167
Hooper, Thomas		Charles Town	W	271-273
Hoover, Conrod	2- Aug [1775?]	St. Mathews Parish	CC	41-42
Hopkins, Henry	20 Feb 1767		X	143-144
Hopkins, John	3 Feb 1777	Congrees, Camden District, St. Marks Parish	BB	29
Hopkins, Thomas	5 Mar 1775	St. Johns Parish	&	515-516
Hopper, James			CC	238
Horn, Alezander	20 Sep 1777	Chs. Town	CC	260-262
Horn, Donald			&	17-18
Horry, John	1 Sep 1770		Y	309-312
Horsburgh, Dr. William			V	57
Hory, Elizabeth	20 Mar 1750/1		B	401
Houslighter, Martin	5 Feb 1767	Orangeburgh	V	143
Houx, Frederick			X	247
Howard, Edward	22 Nov 1750		R(1)	293-295
Howard, Joseph	6 May 1775		&	555
Howard, Robert	7 Jul 1775		&	573
Howard, Robert	16 Aug 1777		BB	71
Howel, Arthur	4 Aug 1753	Congarees	R(2)	47-48
Howel, Bassett	24 Nov 1762		V	313
Howel, Elizabeth	23 Jan 1748/9	Charles Town	B	41-42
Howel, Thomas	23 Jan 1748/9	Charles Town	B	35-41
Howel, William	26 Jul 1757		S	178-179
Howell, Thomas			T	394-395
Hoyl, Jacob	9 Sep 1767	Congaree	X	180-181
Hubbard, John	17 Oct 1769		Y	154-155
Huger, Daniel	30 Jan 1755		R(2)	286-292
Huger, Daniel	1 Apr 1761		T	598-614
Huggins, Geo.	5 Feb 1774		Z	537-539
Huggins, John	30 Mar 1775		&	553
Huggins, Joseph	15 Mar 1762		V	155-157
Hughes, Edward	2 Nov 1772		Z	265
Hughes, Mary widow	12 Apr 1754		R(2)	198-199
Hughes, Thomas	29 & 30 Jan 1761		T	131
Hughes, William	27 Oct 1772		Z	267-270
Hukman, Isaac	3 Feb 1756		T	128
Hulker, John	14 Aug 1750		B	304-305
Hull, Jos.	11 Feb 1768		X	263
Hull, William	29 Sep 1775		&	302-303
Hulme, William	3 Dec 1773	George Town, Black Mingo	AA	123-142
Humbert, David	12 Aug 1769		Y	172-173
Hume, Peter	12 Jan 1746/7		MM	67-69
Hume, Robert	25 Oct 1766	Charles Town	X	122-128
Humphries, Humphry	4 Sep 1777		CC	389-390
Hunscome, Aaron	23 Apr 1761		T	568-569
Hunt, Daniel	-- Sep 1762	St. Philips Parish	V	265-267
Hunt, Mrs. Elizabeth	28 Jan 1767		X	144-146
Hunt, Jos.	3 May 1776		CC	9-10
Hunt, Joseph	11 Dec 1769		Y	166
Hunt, Robert		[two pages only, misnumbered]	R(2)	491-501
Hunt, Samuel	17 May 1754		R(2)	183-185
Hunt, William	Dec 1748		B	27
Hunter, Andrew	9 Dec 1766	Charles Town	W	348-349
Hunter, George			Y	346
Hunter, James	17 Mar 1767	Waccamaw	W	421-423
Hunter, Dr. Joseph			B	212-213
Hunter, Mrs. Mary	3 Mar 1768		X	345-347
Hunter, William	7 Nov 1765	Craven Co.	X	59-60
Hurst, Joseph	15 Dec 1758		T	106-107
Hutchins, Elizabeth	29 Oct 1774	Waccamaw	&	463
Hutchins, John	27 Jan 1755	St. Andrews Parish	R(2)	309-310
Hutchins, John			T	262b-265
Hutchins, John			T	358-359

Name	Date	Location	Vol. & pages	
Hutchins, William	8 Jan 1770		Y	194-195
Hutchinson, Axtal	13 Jun 1764	Granville Co.	W	171
Hutchinson, John	12 May 1759	Granville Co.	T	189-190
Hutchinson, Providence	11 Mar 1756		R(2)	443-445
Hutchinson, Ribson	17 Oct 1757	Charlestown	S	197-207
Hutchinson, William	12 Jan 1774		Z	445-446
Hutchison, John	1 Mar 1768		X	291
Hutson, Rev. William	4 Jul 1761	Charles Town	V	5-8
Hyd, Cornelius	15 Jul 1775	Congrees, St. Marks Parish	BB	23
Hyrne, Burrel Massingbord	11 Jan 1758		S	314-320
Hyrne, Colln. Henry	26 Mar 1764		W	60-63
Ihinger, Michael	28 Nov 1767	High Hill Creek	X	325-326
Imer, Revd. Abraham	20 Nov 1766		W	358-359
Imer, Dr. Frederick	13 Jul 1771	Craven Co.	Z	53-54
Inabinet, John	17 Nov 1773	Orangeburgh Township	Z	447-450
Innes, Nathaniel	3 Mar 1756	Pon Pon	R(2)	449
Ioor, Catherine	18 Sep 1773	Charles Town	Z	391-392
Ioor, John	27 Oct 1772		Z	264-265
Ioor, William	25 Jan 1768	St. Georges Parish	X	240-245
Irby, Edmund	28 Sep 1762		V	272
Irving, James			V	250-251
Irwin, Charles	25 Apr 1755		R(2)	325
Irvin, Edward	23 May 1754		R(2)	225-226
Irwin, John	10 Mar 1772		Z	210-211
Irwin, John	1 Dec 1774		&	493
Irvine, William	2 Feb 1748		MM	293
Isaacs, Solomon	22 Jan 1757		S	62-67
Island, James	28 Aug 1761		V	49
Item, Thomas	6 Mar 1769	St. Helena Parish	Y	52-55
Izard, Mrs. Ann	14 Feb 1755	Granville Co.	R(2)	312-313
Izard, Henry	29 Aug 1749		B	153-158
Izard, John	7 Mar 1754	Prince Williams Parish	R(2)	122-123
Izard, John	14 May 1754		R(2)	190-192
Izard, John	4 Apr 1781	Prince Williams Parish, Granville Co.	BB	217-221
Izard, Joseph			B	179-182
Izard, Ralph	12 Mar 1761	Charles Town	T	507-522
Izard, Walter	3 Jan 1750	Dorchester; Prince Williams Williams Parish	B	375-377
Izard, Walter	20 Feb 1759		T	139-146
Izlar, Jacob	8 Apr 1773	Orangeburgh	Z	341-344
Jackson, Col. George	30 Mar 1775	Colleton Co.	&	530
Jackson, Henery			V	495-497
Jackson, John			MM	334-337
Jackson, John	17 May 1773	Godfreys Savannah	Z	365-367
Jackson, Joseph	26 Jun 1753		R(2)	33
Jackson, Miles			B	330
Jackson, Riginald	7 Mar 1750/1		B	439-441
Jackson, William			T	365-366
Jacobson, Philip	29 Jul 1771		Z	133-135
James, Frances	22 Sep 1762		V	273-275
James, Howell	19 Apr 1773		&	253
James, James	21 Jul 1770	Welch Tract, Craven Co.	Y	299
James, John	16 Aug 1776	Charles Town	BB	1-4
James, Philip			T	486-487
James, Sherwood	1 Jan 1765		W	206
James, William	23 Mar 1751		R(1)	36
James, William	22 Mar 1756	Charles Town(?)	R(2)	437
James, William			V	24
James, William	12 May 1773		&	265
Jameson, William		Black River	W	337-339
Jamieson, James	20 Nov 1772	Craven Co.	&	172
Jamieson, William	25 Oct 1780	Charles Town	BB	202-204; 206
Janviere, Lewis	8 Jun 1748	Charles Town	MM	319-320
Jarvis, Edmund	23 Dec 1762		V	364-365
Jaudon, Daniel	21 Jan 1753		R(1)	531

Name	Date	Location	Vol. & pages	
Jaudon, Daniel	3 May 1763		V	377
Jaudon, Elias	11 Jun 1751		R(1)	21-22
Jaudon, Elisha	1 May 1775	Prince Fredericks Parish	&	559
Jaudon, Paul	14 Mar 1774		Z	539-540
Jeanes, Michael	18 June 1760		T	323-325
Jeanes, Michael			V	251
Jeannerett, Abraham	10 Sep 1756		R(2)	532-534
Jeannerette, Henry	9 Jul 1765	St. Helena Parish	W	270-271
Jeanneratt, Jacob	9 Aug 1749		B	151-152
Jeanneret, John	17 Jan 1775		&	514-515
Jefferson, Joseph	9 Sep 1763	St. John Parish	V	488
Jeffery, William	4 Mar 1775		&	525
Jeffreys, David	29 Apr 1767		W	417-418
Jehne, Doctr. August	21 Nov 1763		V	524-525
Jehne, Mrs. Elizabeth			W	343-344
Jenins, James	6 Nov 1758		T	95-98
Jenkins, Benja.	6 Nov 1782		BB	256-258
Jenkins, Christopher	25 Jan 1760		T	294
Jenkins, Christopher	8-10 Feb 1774		&	371-375
Jenkins, John	23 Jan 1758		S	342-344
Jenkins, John			S	367
Jenkins, John	4 Dec 1764	Edisto Island	W	192-194
Jenkins, Joseph			S	368
Jenkins, Joseph	19 Feb 1771		Y	399-400
Jenkins, Richard	4 Feb 1773	Edisto Island	Z	301-304
Jenkins, Sarah widow			S	367
Jenkins, Sarah	24 Sep 1772	St. Helena Island	Z	259-260
Jenkins, Sarah	25 Apr 1774		&	364-365
Jenkins, William	15 Feb 1758		S	364-367
Jenkins, William			S	368
Jenkins, William	3 Dec 1760		T	462-464
Jenkins, William	7 May 1768		X	305
Jenks, Thomas	13 Jan 1749/50		B	229-230
Jennens, Edward	26 Apr 1765		W	254
Jennens, John	6 Feb 1775	St. James, Santee	AA	70-71
Jenner, John	18 Feb 1775		&	528
Jennings, J[ohn]			B	40
Jennings, Capt. Saml	14 Dec 1750		B	353-354
[Jennis], James	12 Oct 1747	Dorchester	MM	206-207
Jennys, George	2 Jan 1758		S	253-262
Jennys, Mrs. Henrietta	5 May 1759		T	183-184
Jeny, Paul	27 May 1752	Euhaws	R(1)	402-408
Jenys, Thomas	2 Jan 1745/6		MM	140-151
Jerdon, David	10 Jul 1777		CC	209-210
Jerdon, Mary	19 Jul 1764		W	129
Jerman, Ralph	22 Mar 1749		B	247-248
Jernigan, Henry	28 May 1763		V	469-470
Jerusalem, George	19 Mar 1755		R(2)	315-316
Jervey, Jno.	26 Jun 1753		R(2)	33
Jessop, John	7 Nov 1776	St. Pauls Parish	BB	12
Jeter, James			X	42
Jewett, Joseph	6 Aug 1768			
Jinks, John	17 May 1762		V	141-144
Jinnens, Peter	5 Sep 1768		X	392
Jobb, Jacob	3 Dec 1773	Congarees	&	313-314
Johns, Mrs. Mary		St. Johns Parish, Colleton County	S	18-19
Johnson, Abel	19 May 1759		T	190-191
Johnson, James	8 Nov 1751		R(1)	138
Johnson, John	30 Aug 1746	St. Helena, Granll. Co.	MM	38-40
Johnson, John	30 Apr 1753		R(2)	12
Johnson, John	23 Aug 1774	St. Bartholomews Parish	AA	25-27
Johnson, Josiah	30 Apr 1753		R(2)	12-13
Johnson, Richard	21 Jan 1771		Y	428-429
Johnson, Richard	21 Jun 1773	Izards Camp	Z	367-368
[Johnson], Robert	10 Jul 1777	96 District	CC	207
Johnson, Thomas	6 Feb 1746/7	Dorchester	MM	69-70

Name	Date	Location	Vol. & pages	
Johnson, Thomas	8 May 1751	Charles Town	R(1)	1-7
Johnson, Thomas	17 May 1773		&	269-270
Johnson, Thomas	4 Apr 1775	St. Stephens Parish	AA	93
Johnson, Thomas Henry			V	346
Johnson, William	16-25 Mar 1769	Charles Town	Y	90-96
Johnson, William free Negro	25 Feb 1772	St. Bartholomews Parish	&	33
Johnston, Andrew	17 Mar 1764	Charles Town Neck	W	66-71
Johnston, Andrew	8 Oct 1777		CC	265
Johnston, Archibald	16 Dec 1768	George Town	X	424-426
Johnston, David	2 May 1752		R(1)	383
Johnston, Gabriel, late Gov. of N. C.	28 Feb 1752	Charles Town	BB	244
Johnston, George	6 Jul 1761		V	24
Johnston, Joseph	12 Nov 1773		Z	404
Johnston, Samuel	28 & 29 Nov 1776		CC	152-155
Johnston, Sarah widow	10 May 1774	Charles Town	&	380
Johnston, Thomas	27 Jan 1747/8	Dorchester	MM	249-250
Johnston, Wm	29 May 1775	St. Pauls, Chs. Town Dist.	CC	56-59
Johnstone, James	27 Jun 1765	Prince George Parish, Craven Co.	X	39
Joiner, Nathan			AA	36
Joiner, Nehemiah	5 Apr 1781		BB	141
Jolly, Joseph	21 Mar 1764		W	31
Jolly, Ths.	14 Apr ----		Z	548-549
Jones, Mrs. Ann	23 Aug 1768		X	374
Jones, Benjamin	15 May 1760		T	312-314
Jones, Charles	11 Aug 1749		B	164
Jones, Charles	20 Apr 1756		R(2)	434
Jones, Charles			Y	170-171
Jones, Daniel		Ninety Six District	CC	341-342
Jones, Evan	12 Jan 1774	Charlestown	Z	443
Jones, Frederick	29 Jan 1777		CC	160-162
Jones, Henry	10 Aug 1744		R(2)	342
Jones, Henry			S	388-390
Jones, John	22 Apr 1763	Charlestown	V	390-436
Jones, John	16 Mar 1767	Colleton Co.	W	394-395
Jones, John	12 Oct 1774		&	463
Jones, John	25 Jan 1780	St. Bartholomews Parish	BB	269
Jones, John	26 Jan 1778	Ninety Six District	CC	332
Jones, Joseph	6 Mar 1752	Johns Island	R(1)	311-312
Jones, Martha	2 Mar 1750/1		B	421
Jones, Mary Anne	2 Nov 1754		R(2)	268-269
Jones, Maurice	22 Apr 1771		Y	443
Jones, Maurice	22 May 1772		&	59-61
Jones, Philip	6 Sep 1762		V	252-253
Jones, Rachel	21 Feb 1761		T	474-475
Jones, Samuel	7 Jul 1772	St. Peters Parish	Z	232-233
Jones, Sarah	28 Jul 1763		V	476-477
Jones, Mrs. Susanna	30 Nov 1764	Charles Town	W	155
Jones, Thomas	21 Jan 1748/9		B	31
Jones, Thomas	30 Apr 1750		B	248-249
Jones, Thomas	22 May 1777	Ninety Six District	BB	44
Jones, Thomas	13 May 1761		T	617-619
Jones, Thomas	13 Mar 1767		W	416
Jones, Thomas	15 Dec 1766		W	352-353
Jones, Thomas		Granville Co.	Z	114-115
Jones, Capt. Thomas		St. Bartholomews Parish	Z	456-463
Jones, William	8 Sep 1777	St. Bartholomews Parish	CC	254
Jordon, Abraham	13 Mar 1759		T	177-179
Jordan, Basil	18 Sep 1766		W	363-365
Jordan, Bazil	18 Sep 1766		W	335-336
Jordan, Christopher	5 Oct 1764		W	154-155
Jordan, James	3 Jul 1772		&	115-117
Jordan, John	9 Oct 1766		W	339
Jordon, William	25 Nov 1777		CC	300
Jordon, Wm			CC	301
Jorquett, James	13 Apr 1749		B	83-85

Name	Date	Location	Vol. & pages	
Joulee, John	28 Jun 1764	St. Bartholomews Parish, Colleton Co.	W	133-134
Jourdin, Daniel	11 Feb 1760		T	281
Joy, Samuel			W	3
Joy, William	16 Jun 1773	Christ Church Parish	&	270
Joynes, Henry	2 Mar 1761		T	531-532
Jump, William	20 Jul 1761	Berkley Co.	V	36
June, Jno.	29 May 1770		Y	245
June, John	27 May 1774		&	359
June, Peter	16 Aug 1768		X	375-376
June, Soloman	20 Oct 1767		Y	8
June, Stanley	20 Oct 1767		X	211-212
Jurdine, John	26 Jul 1754		S	56-58
Jurdine, Lenard	30 Jan 1778		CC	412
Jurdine, Mary			T	304-305
Kannady, Bryan	11 Jun 1750		B	288
Kavanaugh, Hugh	17 Mar 1773		&	220
Keal, John	19 Mar 1760		T	289
Kean, Garret	29 Apr 1765	Charles Town	W	249-250
Kean, James	1 May 1758		S	390-394
Keating, Maurice	23 Sep 1750		R(1)	46-49
Kechely, Conrad	3 Jul 1764	Charles Town	W	192-198
Keeler, George	18 Aug 1781	St. George's Parish	BB	239-240
Keels, John		Craven Co., Prince Fredericks Parish	V	309-310
Keen, John Junr	21 Jul 1767		X	99
Keen, John Senr	25 Aug 1767		X	160-161
Keir, Revd Patrick	2 Nov 1765		X	128-129
Keis, Henry	-- Apr 1777	Camden District	BB	33
Keith, Rev. Alexander	9 Dec 1772	St. Stephens Parish	&	205-206
Keith, Dr. William	17 Oct 1777	Charlestown	CC	368-369
Keithley, John			T	385-386
Kella, Thomas	22 Aug 1776		CC	33-34
Keller, Paul	23 Sep 1773	Charles Town	Z	426
Keller, Thomas	22 Aug 1776		&	608
Kelly, Daniel	2 Nov 1767		X	212-213
Kelly, John	26 Nov 1766		W	342-343
Kelly, John			Y	395
Kelly, John	23 Feb 1771		Y	396
Kelly, Robt	2 Jun 1750	Charlestown	B	269-270
Kelsall, John	3 Nov 1772	Prince William Parish, Granville Co.	&	162-165
Kemmerland, John George	11 May 1771	Geo: Town, Winyaw	Y	457
Kenedy, William	3 Oct 1754		R(2)	269-270
Kenerly, Thomas	25 Jan 1775		AA	76-77
Kennady, Alexander	17 Nov 1770		Y	381
Kennady, Thos.	18 May 1775		AA	108-109
Kennaston, Samuel	25 Nov 1754	Charles Town	R(2)	273-276
Kennedy, Thomas	21 Nov 1747		MM	211-212
Kentie, John	12 Apr 1771		Y	459
Kerling, George	2 Sep 1774	Jacksonburgh	AA	13
Kerr, Andrew	19 Nov 1772	Long Cane Settlement	Z	288-289
Kerr, John	15 Sep 1761	Craven Co.	V	45
Kerr, John	16 Apr 1771		Y	458
Kerslake, Silas	4 Feb 1754		R(2)	100
Ketchings, Richard	26 Jun 1753		R(2)	33
Kettleband, Daniel	27 Sep 1769		Y	187
Kettles, Jacob		St. Peters Parish	CC	408-409
Kid, James	9 Mar 1768		X	315-316
Kimener, John Martin	31 Jan 1772		Z	162
King, Dinah	1764		W	121
King, Ellington	20 Nov 1773		Z	491
King, Doctor James	6 Feb 1753		R(1)	323-324
King, Jannet			&	563
King, Jannet			AA	111
King, Jasper			B	422-423
King, Jasper	19 Jan 1750/1	Blackmingo, Winyaw	B	424

Name	Date	Location	Vol. & pages	
King, Samuel	6 Nov 1749		B	195-196
King, William	2 May 1764	Williams Burge	W	88
King, William Sr.	16 Nov 1772		Z	266
Kinloch, Francis	14 Dec 1767		X	295-302
Kinloch, Francis	31 Dec 1769	Charles Town	Z	334-338
Kirchner, John	23 Apr 1776		CC	71-73
Kirchner, John	23 Apr 1776	Charles Town	CC	26-27
Kirctmer, John	21 May 1781		BB	177
Kirk, Edward	25 Aug 1774	Charles Town	&	428-429
Kirk, Wm	18 May 1765	Prince Williams Parish	X	33-34
Kirkpatrick, Thomas	27 Dec 1777	Charlestown	CC	274
Kitchens, Charles	25 Nov 1771		&	32-33
Kling, Sabastian	29 Jun 1775		AA	109-111
Knight, John	11 Dec 1776	Johns Island	BB	16-17
Knight, Matthew	24 Sep 1773		Z	390-391
Knight, Thomas	10 Jul 1773		Z	367
Knox, Andrew	14 Feb 1778		CC	329-330
Knott, Jeremiah	21 Feb 1757		S	84-93
Kolb, Henry	1 Nov 1760		T	392-394
Koller, Christian	16 Sep 1766		W	347-348
Koon, Christopher	22 Aug 1768		X	380
Koutts, Jacob	16 May 1777		BB	47-48
Kroyder, George	7 Jan 1764		W	11
Kundall, Thomas	2 Mar 1754	St. Hellener's Parish	R(2)	142-143
Kysell, Conrad	24 Feb 1773	Charles town	Z	397-398
Kysell, Conrad	30 Jan 1773		&	194-198
LaBan, Gabriel			B	259-261
Laban, Gabriel	12 Oct 1752		R(1)	456
Labruce, John	31 Jul 1749		B	158-159
Labruce, Joseph	25 Jul 1764		W	129-130
Lacy, John			T	224-225
Lacy, Samuel	12 Apr 1749		B	82-83
Ladson, Benjamin	15 May 1758		S	403-404
Ladson, Benjamin	11 Mar 1773	St. Helena Island	&	213
Ladson, Mrs. Elizabeth	13 Dec 1780		BB	126-128
Ladson, Francis			R(1)	126-128
Ladson, Francis	19 Dec 1757	St. Andrew Parish	S	237-240
Ladson, Francis	25 May 1770		Y	245-246
Ladson, Henry	16 Aug 1771		Z	84-85
Ladson, Isaac	9 Aug 1774		&	435-437
Ladson, Jacob	17 Jul 1750		B	296-297
Ladson, Jacob	4 Sep 1769	St. Bartholomews Parish	Y	115-117
Ladson, Capt. James			S	371-376
Ladson, John	19 Mar 1770	John's Island	Y	365-366
Ladson, Joseph	1 Feb 1764		W	21-22
Ladson, Joseph	25 May 1768		X	351
Ladson, Mrs. Martha	20 Dec 1751		R(1)	136137
Ladson, Miss Mary	2 Sep 1781	St. Andrews Parish	BB	212-213
Ladson, Robert	21 Mar 1770		Y	233-235
Ladson, Miss Sarah	28 Sep 1773	St. Pauls Parish	Z	441
Ladson, Thomas	1 Mar 1765		W	224-225
Ladson, Major Thomas			S	376-379
Ladson, William			R(2)	426
Ladson, William	16 Feb 1756		R(2)	428-429
Ladson, Zacheus			B	389-390
Ladson, Zacheus	25 Feb 1754		R(2)	109-110
Laing, Samuel	15 Apr 1765		W	246-247
Laird, John	11 Jul 1761	St. Philips Parish, Berkley County	V	77-80
Laird, Patrick	17 Dec 1761	St. Philips Parish	V	97-98
Lamar, Thomas	30 Dec 1776		AA	230-231
Lamboll, Thomas	6 Jan 1775	Charles-town	&	518-522
Lambright, Beltishazzar	31 May 1751		R(1)	43-45
Lambton, Richard	2 May 1777		AA	242-246
Lambwright, Anthony	28 Mar 1765		W	254
Lamond, Robert	22 Mar 1763	Charles Town	V	376-377
Lampard, Biehard	4 Mar 1750/1		B	412

Name	Date	Location	Vol. & pages	
Lampriere, Clement	24 May 1781		BB	179-180
Landall, Robert	15 Jun 1773		Z	358-359
Lander, Fras.	26 Feb 1761		V	61-63
Landgrage, John	10 Jul 1764		W	196
Langley, Mrs. Mary	3 Feb 1764		W	13-14
Langresh, John	31 Jan 1776	Chs Town	CC	60
Lankaster, William	23 Jun 1762		V	467
Lansac, Susanna	17 Jul 1749		B	132
Lapeir, Paul	20 May 1752		R(1)	380-383
Lapier, Paul Sr	3 May 1753		R(2)	64-65
Lapp, John George	25 Feb 1777		BB	32
Lardant, Mary	9 Feb 1758		S	350
Larken, Edmund			R(2)	2
Laroche, John			V	194-195
Laroche, Mary	16 Feb 1760		T	282-283
Larry, Michael	2 Oct 1759		T	274-276
Lary, Peter			R(2)	285-286
LaTour, Charlotte	1 Jul 1756		R(2)	490
Laurence, James	12 Feb 1768	WilliamsBurgh	X	267-268
Laurence, Rachael	16 Apr 1767	Charles Town	W	411-412
Laurence, Richard Dunn	17 Feb 1758		S	379-381
Laurens, Augustus	-- May 1758		S	439-442
Laurens, John	11 Sep 1745	Charles Town	MM	176-191
Laurens, Peter	20 Nov 1747	Charles Town	MM	207-208
Lawrence, John			V	354-355
Lawson, John			T	401-402
Lawton, Jeremiah	20 May 1762		V	241
Lawton, Josiah	20 Dec 1757		S	324-325
Lawton, William	19 Dec 1757		S	289-296
Lavington, Samuel	27 Feb 1764	Colleton Co., St. Bartholomews Parish	W	53-54
Leacraft, John	23 Nov 1771	Charles Town	Z	135
Leaton, Richard	8 & 10 Dec 1759		T	266-267b
LeBarron, Francis	29 Jun 1774	George Town	&	325-326
LeBarron, Francis	8 Dec 1773		&	326-327
Leber, Samuel	21 Mar 1774			
Lecraft, John	18 Sep 1758		T	45-46
Lee, Thomas	5 Sep 1769		Y	149-151
Legare, Solomon	10 Dec 1774		AA	71-72
Legare, Solomon Senr	26 Mar 1761		T	493
Leger, John	9 Apr 1765	Prince Fredericks Praish	X	27-28
Leger, Peter Senior		Charles Town	V	105-107
Leger, Samuel	16 Jun 1752		R(1)	419-420
Legrand, Isaac	27 Jul 1762		V	244-245
Legrand, Isaac	23 Feb 1781		BB	117
Legueux, Peter	8 Apr 1772		&	76-78
Lehre, John	16 Feb 1768		X	280
Leigh, Hon. Peter	18 Sep 1759		T	254-259
Leitch, Thomas	10 Dec 1767		X	245
LeJau, Francis	5 Nov 1765	St. Johns Parish	Y	28-31
LeJau, Francis	24 Apr 1773		&	234-243
Lennon, Thomas	9 Nov 1773	Orangeburgh	Z	415-416
Lenud, Albert	10 Mar 1765	Prince Frederick Parish	W	242-243
Lepear, Paul	21 Apr 1756		R(2)	468-469
Lesesne, Francis	31 May 1770		Y	244
Lesesne, Isaac	25 Jul 1773		Z	247-250
Lesley, Charles	13 Sep 1753		R(2)	50
Leslie, Chas.	22 Mar 1762		V	194
Lessene, Mrs. Elizabeth	14 & 16 Aug 1775		CC	42-46
Lessesne, John	23 Aug 1771		Z	86-87
Lever, Jacob	3 --- 1762	Congaree Fork	V	184-185
Lewes, Henry	19 Feb 1761		T	497-498
Lewis, Charles	15 May 1770	All Saints Parish	Y	275-278
Lewis, Charlotte spinster	15 Apr 1756	Prince Georges Parish	R(2)	473-474
Lewis, Daniel	11 Mar 1774		Z	510
Lewis, Jenkin			S	354-355
Lewis, James	20 May 1765		W	261-262

Name	Date	Location	Vol. & pages	
Lewis, John		Charles Town	R(2)	66-67
Lewis, John	30 Nov 1768	St. James Santee, Craven County	X	405
Lewis, John	14 Apr 1777	Beaufort	AA	187-188
Lewis, Ledgwick		St. James Goosecreek & St. Johns	&	528-529
Lewis, Mary	1 Jan 1756	Catfish	R(2)	407
Lewis, Stephen	14 Jan 1774		Z	494
Lewis, Thomas	27 Jul 1773	Berkley Co.	&	301
Lewis, William	7 Apr 1781		BB	147-148
Liddle, Capt. Archibald	21 Nov 1747		MM	238-239
Liddle, James	15 Apr 1760		T	306-307
Lide, John	10 May 1764		W	142-144
Lightbody, Robert	17 Feb 1781		BB	154
Lightwood, Edward Sr.	15 Nov 1769		Y	157-159
Liles, Ephraim	7 Apr 1767		W	418-420
Lind, Thomas		Charles Town	&	94-99
Linde, Moses	17 May 1774	Charles Town	&	591-592
Linder, Ludowix	21 Aug 1761		T	30-32
Lindfors, Charles Jacob	9 Dec 1776	St. Georges Parish	&	643
Lindsay, Patrick	18 Mar 1747		B	21
Lindsey, Thomas			B	361
Lingard, James	12 Dec 1770		Y	406-408
Lingard, James	28 Dec		Z	14-15
Lining, Thos.		Charles Town	V	525-528
Linn, David	27 Jan 1775	Wandow	&	517-518
Linn, James	27 Apr 1776	Camden Dist.	CC	374-375
Linnen, Thomas	19 May 1772		&	135
Linton, John	9 Aug 1774	St. Helena Parish	AA	2-3
Linus, Ann	17 Sep 1770		Y	313
Linus, James			R(1)	401-402
Linus, Moses	29 Sep 1767	St. Georges Parish	X	252-253
Linus, Moses	18 Sep 1770	St. George	Y	312-313
Liston, Robert			T	337-338
Little, Saml	14 Oct 1765	Berkley Co., St. Johns Parish	Y	26
Little, Wm.	10 Jul 1753		R(2)	48-49
Little, William	18 Dec 1767		X	231-233
Livingston, George	16 Jul 1766		W	305
Livingston, George	20 Jan 1769		X	431-432
Livingston, Henry Junior	6 Mar 1765		W	241-242
Livingston, Hugh	11 Aug 1758		T	41-42
Livingston, Jno	8 Jan 1774		&	473
Livingston, Wm Smilie	2 Dec 1772	Colleton Co.	&	172-173
Livre, Alexander	4 May 1756	Charles town	R(2)	450-451
Lloyd, Caleb	27 Mar 1767		W	411
Lloyd, Dr. Henry	Feb 1770	Edistoe Island	Y	223-224
Lloyd, John	11 Dec 1770	Amelia Township	Y	355-356
[Lloyd, Capt. John]	10 Jan 1759		T	180-183
Lloyd, Major John		Barkley Co.	&	36
Lloyd, Mrs. Martha	7 Mar 1771		Y	408-409
Lloyd, Mrs. Mary	5 Mar 1764		W	24
Lloyd, William	9 Dec 1761	Chs. Town	V	73-74
Lochon, Vivien	27 Mar 1773	Charles Town	Z	311-312
Lockhart, Jno.	11 Nov 1777	Camden Dist.	CC	317-318
Logan, George	25 Oct 1773		Z	401-402
Long, Alexr.	19 Mar 1763		V	441
Long, Georg	13 Feb 1775	St. Bartholomews Parish	&	512
Lonsdale, Rev. Mr. [William]	2 Apr 1767	Prince Williams Parish	X	86-87
Loocok, Doctor William	30 Nov 1781	Charles Town	BB	231-234
Lopha, Matthias	5 Aug 1771		Z	132
Lord, Anthony	26 May 1774		&	400-401
Lord, Jas.	27 Sep 1764		W	170
Lorimer, Jane	1 Jan 1753	Charles Town	R(1)	532
Lorimore, James	26 Sep 1763		W	264
Lormier, Lewis	-- Jan 1747/8		MM	240
Love, Jacob	18 Sep 1777		AA	262

Name	Date	Location	Vol.	& pages
Love, Jacob	18 Sep 1777		CC	240
Love, James	17 Jun 1760		T	340-341
Loveday, Sarah			X	82
Lovekin, Roger	29 Sep 1753	Granville Co., St. Helena	R(2)	78-79
Loveless, John	4 May 1769	Peedee	X	460-461
Loveless, Thomas	15 Mar 1748		MM	329
Lowles, Samuel	27 Jun 1759		T	239
Lowndes, Charles	28 Jul 1763	Charles Town	V	479-482
Loyabrumby, Thomas	22 Jun 1767		Y	32-33
Loyer, Adrian	9 Apr 1750		B	241
Lucas, Thomas	10 Jul 1769		Y	101
Luther, Peter			W	331
Lydston, Gidion	23 Apr 1750		B	262-263
Lykes, George	22 Nov 1775		AA	122
Lynch, Sabina	21 Mar 1748		MM	295-297
Lynch, Thomas	28 Feb 1778		CC	346-352
Lynch, Col. Thomas			MM	298
Lynn, Valentine	7 Sep 1781		BB	226-227
Lyon, John	6 Sep 1781	Charles Town	BB	206-207
Lyon, Redman	22 Feb 1772		&	31
McAlexander, Nathaniel			R(2)	228-229
McAlpine, Capt. Coll	15 Feb 1773		&	259
McAlpine, James	15 May 1775		CC	51-56
McBrid, John	23 Oct 1767		X	294
McBride, John	19 Feb 1767	Williamsburgh, Craven Co.	X	60-61
McCall, Thos	27 Feb 1781	Stono Ferry	BB	110-112
McCalla, William	8 Nov 1758		T	104
McCants, James	3 Apr 1772	Prince Fredericks Parish	&	93-94
McCants, John	1 Jul 1772		&	128-130
McCants, William	2 Aug 1763		V	484-486
McCartey, William	22 May 1750	New Windsor	B	297-298
McCarty, Daniel	14 Dec 1762		V	337-338
Macauley, Alexander			T	498-501
McCauley, Hugh	16 Mar 1775		&	530
McCautry, Robert	9 Jun 1752		R(1)	393-394
McCawley, William	2 Aug 1764		W	172-173
McClauchlin, John	1 Jun 1762		V	234
McCleland, James		Williamsburgh	V	67
McClellan, William	10 Jan 1772		Z	207
McClendon, Mary	15 May 1771	Craven [Co.]	Z	127
McClinckey, Alexander	3 Jul 1752		R(1)	421
McCluer, John	16 Jun 1767		W	446-447
McCluer, William	25 Oct 1749		B	227-228
McClure, James	24 Oct 1771	Craven Co.	Z	135-136
McCoard, John	13 Apr 1772		Z	226-227
McConnell, John	2 Sep 1752		R(1)	451
McCord, Capt. John	8 Aug 1768	Craven Co.	X	403-404
McCormack, John	4 Mar 1750/1		B	399-400
McCormick, Wm.	16 Nov 1750		B	368
McCormick, Nathaniel	22 Dev 1764		W	27-28
McCoun, James [?]	2 May 1751		R(1)	23
McCoy, Hugh			R(1)	347
McCoy, John	25 Oct 1769		Y	137
McCracken, Robert	18 Apr 1774		&	340
McCrea, James	21 Mar 1771	Craven Co., Williamsburgh Township	Y	427
McCrea, John	24 Jul 1765	Craven Co., Prince Fredericks Parish	X	42-43
McCrea, Joseph	12 May 1763	Black Mingo, Craven Co.	V	372-373
McCrea, Thomas	18 May 1777	Craven Co., Williamsburgh Township	BB	34-35
McCree, Thomas	2 May 1750		B	266
McCulloch, Elizabeth	21 Jan 1777		AA	176-177
McCulloch, Hance	25 Jul 1769		Y	102
McCullough, John Senr	19 May 1761		V	10-11
McCullough, William	30 Dec 1774		&	492
McCully, James	19 Feb 1774		Z	493

Name	Date	Location	Vol. & pages	
McCutchen, Hugh	30 Nov 1769	Craven Co.	Y	172
McCutchen, William	9 Jul 1770		Y	443
McDaniel, Daniel			Z	83
McDaniel, Thos			S	58-60
McDonald, Daniel	6 Feb 1768		X	266
McDonald, Daniel	8 Dec 1777	Craven Co., Camden Dist.	CC	355
McDonald, John	26 Jan 1771		Y	384-385
McDonald, John	18 Jan 1763		V	336
McDonald, Reynold	3 Oct 1770		Y	344-345
McDonogh, Cap'n Terence	3 Feb 1774	Charles Town	&	314
McDowall, Dr. Alexander	3 Oct 1765		X	140-141
McDowall, Hough			T	586-588
McDowell, Christopher	5 Dec 1764		W	190
McDowell, Elizabeth	30 Dec 1761		V	86
McDowell, Fergus			W	139-140
McDowell, Isabella	22 Nov 1768		X	397-398
McEhenny, Thomas	16 Jul 1776	St. Marks Parish	CC	14
McElroy, Mary	29 Jul 1751		R(1)	62-63
McEwen, Daniel	29 May 1753		R(2)	16
McFaclan, Capt. George	14 Feb 1781		BB	113
McGarrack, Hugh	16 May 1765		X	30-31
McGaw, James	28 Jan 1756	Christ Church Parish	R(2)	413
McGill, Hugh	21 Dec 1753	Williamsburgh	R(2)	84
McGill, Hugh	10 Apr 1761		T	537
McGill, John	20 Jul 1768		X	411
McGillivray, Alexander	23 Jan 1764		W	8-9
McGillvery, Alexander	12 Feb 1757		S	53-55
McGillivray, Farchur	30 Mar 1771	Charles Town	Y	446
McGinny, Wm.			CC	266-267
McGowen, James	20 Jan 1759		T	108
McGowen, John	25 Feb 1765	St. Johns Parish	W	237-238
McGregory, Alexander	15 Sep 1755	Charles Town	R(2)	363
McGregory, Danl	3 Apr 1770		Y	299-301
McGregory, Daniel	23 Mar 1759		T	199
McGregor, James	22 Mar 1774		Z	528
McGrew, Alexander	2 May 1777		BB	41
McGrigore, Mrs. Martha	4 Jul 1750	St. Thomas & St. Dennis Parish	B	320-321
McGuire, William	8 Dec 1773	Prince Williams Parish	Z	431-432
McHaffey, Oliver	27 Sep 1768		Y	38
McHelvey, Jame			T	402
McHugh, Peter	28 Feb 1757		S	38
McHugo, William	25 Sep 1773		Z	390
McIntire, Daniel	29 Aug 1776	Charles Town	AA	154
McIntosh, Hugh	5 Aug 1768		X	365
McIntosh, John	11 May 1747	Pallichowlas	MM	101-103
McIver, John	1 Jul 1755		R(2)	352
McIver, Rodrick	26 Oct 1775		CC	47-48
McKay, Mr.	2 Feb 1754		R(2)	98-99
McKay, Charles	25 Nov 1776	St. Marks Parish	BB	11
McKee, Allen	8 Jun 1781		BB	178-179
McKee, Archabald	23 May 1777	Prince Fredericks Parish	BB	40
McKee, David	14 Dec 1775		CC	2-4
McKee, David Junr	29 Oct 1773		Z	411-412
McKee, John	31 Mar 1750	George Town	B	247
McKee, John Sr.	9 Apr 1771		Y	452-453
Mackelvey, Alexander	12 Nov 1747		MM	249
McKelvey, Robt	9 Mar 1774		&	336
McKelvy, James	8 Feb 1754	Berkley Co.; Craven Co.	R(2)	144-149
McKelvy, James	3 Apr 1777		CC	384-385
McKelvy, James & Margaret		St. Johns, Berkley	CC	396-398
McKelvey, Mrs. Margaret	1 May 1754		R(2)	181
McKelvey, William	14 Jun 1768		X	374-375
McKenny, Andrew	2 Jan 1758		S	281-282
Mackenzie, Alexander	29 Sep 1781	Charles Town	BB	213
M'Kenzie, Alexander	24 Feb 1778	St. Mathews Parish, Camden Dist.	CC	403-404

Name	Date	Location	Vol. & pages	
McKenzie, Donald	27 Nov 1780		BB	170-171
McKenzie, John	31 May 1758		S	408-412
McKenzie, John	10 Aug 1771	Charles Town	Z	64-74
[McKewn, Andrew]	7 Dec 1769		Y	171
McKewn, John	14 Apr 1777		AA	223
Mackewn, Robert Junr	13 May 1765		W	319-321
McKey, Rev. David	30 Apr 1770	Williamsburgh	Y	233
Mckey, Jon.	24 Dec 1770		Y	403-404
McKinley, John	8 Jan 1772		Z	199-200
[McKinney], Hugh			T	462
McKinnie, Benjamin	20 Jan 1760		T	280-281
Mackintosh, Hugh	12 Dec 1770		Y	391
McKlveen, John	28 Jul 1772		Z	240-241
McKnight, John	Feb 1750/1		B	401
McKnight, Thomas	25 Oct 1776		AA	148
McKrea, Captain James	31 Mar 1757		S	95-97
McLahan, Robert			B	242
McLane, Allen	15 Jul 1751		R(1)	85-86
McLane, Charles	8 Mar 1759		T	162
McLaren, Jas:	18 Oct 1770		Y	332-334
McLaughling, James	30 Jan 1762		T	460-462
Mclaughling, James	23 Feb 1774	St. Pauls Parish	Z	500-504
Mclaughling, William	26 Feb 1773		Z	316-326
McLean, Allen	16 Mar 1762	Prince Williams Parish	V	117-118
McLean, Allen	5 Jan ----	Granville Co.	V	505
McLeod, John	8 May 1771	Prince Williams Parish	Y	452
McLeod, John	27 Oct 1769		Y	151-153
Maclimore, Richard	15 Jul 1772	St. Davids Parish	&	264-265
McLynchey, William			&	545-546
McMahan, Edward	23 Sep 1766		W	334-335
McMahan, John	1766		W	297-298
McMarth, John	11 Apr 1774		&	338
McMasters, Andrew	2 Oct 1764		W	155-157
McMekham, Andrew	13 Jun 1777		CC	255-256
McMullen, Nathaniel	4 Feb 1765	Craven Co., WilliamsBurgh	W	223
McMurdy, John	18 Jul 1758		T	39
McMurdy, Robert	21 Feb 1759		T	168-169
[McNash], John	13 Apr 1748		MM	298-299
McNealy, Jas.	20 Feb 1764		W	18-19
McNeill, Docr. Archibald	4 Jul 1774		AA	17-19
McNichol, George	26 Mar 1754	Craven Co.	R(2)	149-150
McNichol, George	30 Dec		W	289-290
McNichol, John	18 Jul 1771		Z	55-57
McNight, William	17 Jul 1764	Williams Burg	W	172
McPharson, Dougall	29 Oct 1771	Beaufort, Port Royall	Z	125
McPherson, James	2 Jun 1761		T	627-629
McPherson, James	16 Sep 1776		AA	149
McPherson, Capt. James	9 Apr 1771	Prince Williams Parish	Y	450-452
McPherson, James Jr.	6 May 1762		V	208-209
McPherson, Jane	7 Jul 1764	Prince Williams Parish	W	128-129
Mcpherson, John	13 Apr 1747	Charles Town	MM	124-126
[McPherson], John	20 Mar 1763		V	374-376
McPherson, Joshua	13 Aug 1774	Prince Wms Parish, Beaufort	&	454-455
Mcpherson, Lydia	Sep 177-		CC	233
McPherson, Thomas	27 Apr 1767		W	408-409
McPherson, William	17 Feb 1749/50		B	221-222
McQueen, John	28 Jan 1764		W	159-167
McRee, Deborah	8 Mar 1757		S	141-142
McRee, Deborah	8 Jan 1759		T	104-105
McRee, Captain James	8 Mar 1757		S	93-95
McTaddian, John	23 Sep 1776	Prince Fredericks Parish	AA	148
McTeer, Mrs. Hannah	8 Feb 1771	Prince Williams Parish	Y	395-396
Mcteer, John	26 Jul 1754		R(2)	129
McTeer, Will	23 Apr 1768	Prince Williams Parish	X	331-332
McWarter, John			V	198-199
McWherter, Hance			&	309-311
Mace, Thomas	7 Jun 1773		Z	445

Name	Date	Location	Vol. & pages	
Maher, Matthew	13 May 1768		X	352
Maine, William	31 Jan 1777	Prince William's Parish	AA	189-190
Makey, Roger	10 Dec 1777		CC	307
Mallen, James	22 & 23 Dec 1772		&	187
Mallet, Daniel	8 Oct 1776		CC	127-128
Mallets, Gidion	9 Mar 1771		Y	429
Maltby, Rev. John	5 Feb 1772	Willtown, St. Pauls Parish	&	20-22
Man, John	5 Jun 1755		R(2)	370-371
Maner, William		Stevens Creek	&	414
Maner, Wm	25 Aug 1774	St Peters Parish	&	447
Manigault, Peter	14 Feb 1774	Goose creek	&	402-414
Maning, Jethro			X	294
Maning, Robert		St. Lukes Parish	Z	41-42
Manley, James	9 Jan 1765		W	204-205
Manly, Ann	14 Jan 1782		BB	242
Mann, Henry	25 Dec 1773		Z	516-517
Manning, Mrs. Sarah			B	403
Manning, Mrs. Sarah	8 May 1777		BB	68
Mannon, Aaron	4 Jun 1774		&	333-334
Manrow, Daniel	12 Jul 1766		W	296
Maples, Thos	18 Dec 1777		CC	278
Marion, Benjamin	1 Dec 1750		B	353
Marion, James	3 Mar 1769		Y	42-44
Marion, Gabriel	25 Apr 1777		BB	52-55
Marley, John	12 Mar 1773		Z	504-507
Maronzy, Julian	14 Oct 1767		Y	8-9
Marr, Andrew	23 Feb 1781	Chas. Town	BB	114-116
Marriot, Lancelot	-- May 1747		MM	97
Marsh, James	20 Jul 1757	St. Philips Parish	S	184-189
Marshall, Alexander	10 Nov 1747	Charles Town	MM	201-202
Marshall, George		St. Phillips Parish	X	254-256
Marshall, Isabel	27 Apr 1767		Y	125-127
Marshall, [James]	[20 Oct 1764]	Charlestown	W	462-464
Marshall, Capt Robert	6 Aug 1750	Charles Town	B	301
Marson, William	19 Jan 1778	Prince Fredericks Parish	CC	401
Martin, Abraham	3 Oct 1774		AA	33-34
Martin, Bassack	24 Jan 1753		R(1)	502-503
Martin, Isaac	30 Jun 1749	Ponpon	B	131
Martin, Jacob	5 Dec 1760		T	436
Martin, [James]		St. Bartholomews Parish	MM	275-277
Martin, James	26 Jan 1749/50	Ponpon	B	226
Martin, James	8 Apr 1749		B	89-91
Martin, John	27 Jul 1753	Charles Town	R(2)	72-73
Martin, John	27 Nov 1771		&	31-32
Martin, John			&	3
Martin, Thomas	25 Dec 1770	Craven Co.	Y	423
Martinangle, Philip	6 Oct 1761		V	68-69
Mashow, Henry	24 May 1759		T	213-214
Mathewes, Benjamin	18 Jun 1755	Charles Town	R(2)	459-461
Mathewes, James	26 Feb 1745/6		MM	243-246
Mathewes, John	23 Jan 1760	Charles Town	T	308-309
Mathewes, Sarah			T	397-398
Mathews, Christiana	13 Mar 1752		R(1)	343-344
Mathews, George	-- Mar 1771	Berkley Co.	Y	378
Mathews, James	19 Feb 1767	St. Philips Parish	W	392-393
Mathews, John	18 May 1750	St. Thomas & St. Denis Parish	B	286
Mathews, John	24-25 May 1751		R(1)	14
Mathews, John	3 Dec 1776	Charlestown	AA	162-167
Mathews, John	11 Jun 1750		B	285
Mathews, William	15 Nov 1773		Z	404-406
Mathin, John	23 May 1777	Beaufort	CC	198-199
Matthews, Anthony	21 Jul 1769	Johns Island	Y	86-87
Matthews, George	[1769]	Charles Town	Y	62-66
Matthews, James	22 Jan 1744/5	Johns Island	MM	193-195
Matthews, Mrs. Lois	5 Feb 1753		R(1)	508-509
Matthews, William	7 Oct 1754	Granville Co.	R(2)	272
Matthews, William	20 Jan 1769		Y	56-59

Name	Date	Location	Vol. & pages	
[Matthisen], Abraham	6 May 1748		MM	299-300
Maverick, Samuel	15 Jun 1758		T	37-38
May, James	30 Sep 1767		Y	33-34
May, John	13 Nov 1765		W	340-341
May, Mrs. Martha	23 Jan 1773		&	199-201
May, William	15 Jun 1758		T	27-30
Maybank, David	10 Jun 1767		X	115-118
Mayll, William Hope	23 Feb 1754		R(2)	157-158
Mayrant, John	30 Jun 1767		X	163-166
Mays, Richard			AA	151
Mazyck, Paul	28 Oct 1750	Berkley Co.	B	299-301
Mazyck, Stephen	1 Jan 1771	Berkley Co.	Z	101-105
Mazyck, William		Charles Town	&	585-590
Means, James	2 May 1772		&	169-172
Meisner, John Frederick	4 Feb 1762		V	90-91
Mell, Thomas Senr	12 Jan 1760		T	273-274
[Mellet, Peter]	13 Jul 1764		W	177
Mellicham, Thomas	29 Apr 1774		&	324-325
Mellicham, Thomas	25 Jul 1781	Stono	BB	183
Melven, Thomas	29 Dec 1770	Colleton Co., St. Bartholomews Parish	Y	358-350
Melvill, David	26 May 1767		W	460
Merkley, Frederick	13 Jul 1759		T	214-215
Matheringham, Mrs. Eliz.	3 Mar 1758		T	3-8
Metzger, Henry	6 Jan 1776		CC	332-333
Meyer, Dr. Nicholas Frederick	27 Aug 1774		&	455-458
Michau, Capt. Abraham	8 Jan 1774		Z	473
Michau, Abraham Senior	27 May 1767		W	395-396
Michau, Peter		Prince Fredericks Parish, Craven Co.	Z	252-253
Michie, Alexander	13 Sep 1774	St. Michaels Parish	AA	30-33
Michie, Hon. James	22 Nov 1760		T	445-453
Michie, William	21 Feb 1772	Charles Town	Z	174
Mickells, Valentine	16 Oct 1770		Y	332
Middleton, Richard	31 Dec 1750	Craven Co.	R(1)	355-356
Middleton, Mrs. Sarah	27 Nov 1765		X	197-203
Middleton, Thomas	-- May 1747		MM	96
Middleton, Thomas			MM	240-241
Middleton, Thomas	13 Feb 1767		W	397-403
Middleton, Thomas	7 & 8 Dec 1768	Granville Co.	X	414-419
Middleton, William	24 Apr 1773		Z	340
Miers, Jasper	14 Jun 1777	St. Bartholomews Parish, Colleton County	CC	191
Miers, John	14 Jul 1772		&	187-189
Mikel, James	2 May 1772	St. Davids Parish	&	73
Mikell, John	4 May 1765		W	258
Milas, Thomas	29 May 1756		R(2)	451-453
Miles, Allan	19 Oct 1780		BB	96-97
Miles, Edward	22 Nov 1765		X	194-195
Miles, Edward	16 Mar 1773	Charles Town	Z	315
Miles, Edward	4 Mar 1774	St. Andrews Parish	Z	499-500
Miles, James	12 Feb 1774		Z	535-537
Miles, Jeremiah			T	205-206
Miles, John	16 Apr 1773	Charles Town	Z	332-334
Miles, John Sr.	22 Jul 1773	Horsavanna	Z	392-394
Miles, Joseph Capt.	19 Feb 1771		Y	411-414
Miles, Mary			W	230-232
Miles, Moses			Y	434
Miles, Capt. Silas	2 Feb 1767	Charles Town	X	135-138
Miles, Capt. Silas	15 May 1772	Charles Town	Z	212-222
Miles, Thomas	2 Dec 1757		S	267-269
Miles, Thomas	25 Apr 1761		T	620-621
Miles, Capt. Thomas	2 Jun 1757		S	169-174
Miles, William	25 Aug 1752	St. Bartholomews Parish, Colleton Co.	R(1)	481-486
Miles, William			T	341-345
Miles, William	2 Jul 1764	Horse Savanah, St. Pauls Parish	W	134-138

Name	Date	Location	Vol. & pages	
Miles, William	2 Jul 1764	Horse Savannah, St. Pauls Parish	W	134-138
Miles, William	18 Aug 1774	St. Andrews Parish	&	432-434
Milhouse, Robert	6 Jan 1756	Fredericksburgh Township	R(2)	405
Milhouse, Robert	20 Dec 1771		Z	204-205
Milhouse, Samuel	9 Jan 1777		CC	149-152
Mill, Charles	13 Aug 1772		Z	240
Miller, Mr.	20 Jan 1752		R(1)	312-314
Miller, Barbara	26 Aug 1760		T	494
Miller, Barbary	27 Aug 1760		T	383-385
Miller, David	27 Dec 1746		MM	66-67
Miller, David	29 Apr 1755		R(2)	342-343
Miller, Mrs. Elizabeth	1 Jul 1762	St. Georges Parish	V	233
Miller, Jacob	27 Oct 1764		W	153
Miller, Jacob	14 May 1768		X	326-327
Miller, Jacob	17 Aug 1772	Craven Co., St. Davids Parish	Z	254-255
Miller, Jacob	8 Sep 1772	Craven Co.	Z	338-339
Miller, John			B	87-88
Miller, John	16 Dec 1776		BB	7-8
Miller, John	16 Sep 1777	Ninety Six District	CC	275-276
Miller, Moses	-- Feb 1747/8		MM	266-267
Miller, Robert	9 Mar 1765		W	232-233
Miller, Robert			&	307-308
Miller, Samuel	29 Nov 1758		T	123-124
Miller, Stephen	1 Feb 1749/50		B	222-224
Miller, Colln. Stephen	28 Sep 1776	St. Thomas Parish	CC	140-148
Miller, Doctr. Thomas	23 Dec 1774		&	508-509
Milligan, James	14 Apr 1777		CC	176-183
Mills, George	17 Apr 1775		&	590
Mills, Robert	13 Sep 1768		X	399
Mills, Robert	17 Feb 1770	Charlestown	Y	192-194
Milnar, Samuel		Charles Town	V	70
Milner, Job	4 Feb 1763		V	543-545
Milner, John	16 Dec 1749		B	208-210
Milner, Mrs. Mary	28 Mar 1777	Christ Church Parish	CC	213-216
Milner, Solomon	22 Dec 1757	Johns Island; Charlestown	S	310-314
Milvin, Thomas Jr.	19 May 1769		X	456-457
Minors, Charles	16 Apr 1770		Y	225
Minors, Robert			W	223-224
[Miot], Alexander	28 Sep 1772		Z	266-267
Miscampbell, James	1 Dec 1777	long cane	CC	335-336
Miskell, Ephraim	19 Apr 1767		W	393
Misman, John Ludwick	18 May 1776		CC	5-6
Mitchel, Dr. George	7 Feb	Jacksonburgh	B	237-240
Mitchel, James			X	420
Mitchel, John	13 Mar 1750/1		B	402
Mitchel, Moses	4 Oct 1776		&	620-621
Mitchel, Thomas	15 Apr 1768	Prince Georges Parish	X	286-289
Mitchell, Hannah	31 Feb 1758		S	329
Mitchell, John	12 Feb 1767	George Town	Y	1-2
Mitchell, John Roe	29 Dec 1774		AA	69-70
Mitchell, Meriam	13 Dec 1777		CC	395-396
Mitchell, Robert	26 Sep 1777	96 District	CC	242-243
Mitchell, Sarah			V	146
Mitchell, William	10 Jul 1762		AA	[following p.83
Mitchell, William	10 Jul 1762		AA	265
Mitchison, William	2 Jul 1761	Craven Co.	V	29
Moat, Jonathan	15 Feb 1763		V	363
Moffet, Solomon	16 Jan 1768		X	234-235
Molly--free Mulatto child	16 Sept 1772		&	166
Monaghan, David	16 Oct 1776	St. Davids Parish	AA	157
Monck, Tho.	8 Mar 1757/8	Colleton Co.	MM	300-301
Monclar, Amy	20 Mar 1752	Charles Town	R(1)	322-323
Monclar, Peter	4 Mar 1777		AA	176
Mongin, David			Y	430-431
Mongin, Marian	16 Jan 1772		Z	161-162
Monk, George	3 Feb 1772	Prince Georges Parish	&	9

Name	Date	Location	Vol. & pages	
Monk, John	6 Jun 1750		B	272-273
Monk, Saml	6 Apr 1772	St. Stephens Parish	&	49
Monk, Thomas			W	91
Monk, William	10 Feb 1772	Prince Georges Parish	Z	176-177
Montgomery, Alexander	27 Mar 1767		W	438-439
Montgomery, George	2 Sep 1758		T	39-40
Montgomery, Henry	7 Mar 1777	Craven Co.	BB	37
Montgomery, Henry	2 Mar 1769	Craven Co., Williamsburgh Township	Y	38-39
Montgomery, Rebecca	1 Feb 1750		T	112
Montgomery, William	25 Mar 1771		Y	425
Moody, Mrs. Catherine		Charles Town	Y	354
Moody, Joseph	8 Nov 1770	Charles Town	Y	354-355
Moon, Duncan	12 Sep 1767	Granl. Co., Prince Wm Parish	Y	34
Moon, James	21 Feb 1772		&	18-19
Moor, John		Williamsburgh	B	418
Moore, Francis			Z	99-100
Moore, Francis	17 Jan 1772		&	72-73
Moore, James	23 Nov 1772		&	174-175
Moore, James	28 Jan 1775		AA	79
Moore, James Weems	23 Aug 1773	Prince Williams Parish, Jacksonburgh	Z	396
Moore, John	29 Aug 1761	St. Peters Parish, Granville Co.	V	65-67
Morf, Jacob	7 Dec 1762		V	317-319
Moore, Michael	3 Oct 1752		R(1)	453
Moore, Richard	7 Nov 1765		X	209
Moraine, Edward Jr.			W	10
Morand, Francis	7 Oct 1766		W	325-327
Morgan, James	27 Oct 1777	Charlestown	CC	273-274
Morgan, John			W	334
Morgan, John	20 May 1772		Z	236-237
Morgan, Purchase	27 Mar 1777		AA	186
Morgan, Rev. Thomas	15 Nov 1769	Charles Town	Y	217-218
Morgan-Dollar, Kasper	18 May 1767		W	432-434
Morison, John			T	392
Morison, Mrs. Mary	9 Jun 1766		W	406-407
Morobray, Thomas	14 Feb 1767	St. Helenas Parish	X	160
Morrall, Daniel	10 Apr 1772	Waccamaw	&	46-47
Morrall, Capt. Jno.	21 Feb 1771		Y	423-425
Morrell, Francis	15 Nov 1751	Berkley Co.	R(1)	129-130
Morris, Mark	9 Mar 1781		BB	149-150
Morrison, Robert	26 Dec 1768	Craven Co.	X	413
Mortimer, Edward	4 & 11 Mar 1772		Z	209-210
Mortimer, Edward	24 Jul 1771	Monks Corner	Z	78-82
Mortimer, Richard	1 May 1758		S	386-387
Morton, John	9 Jan 1752		R(1)	285-289
Motte, Isaac	26 May 1753		R(2)	171-173
Motte, Jacob Sr.	19 Jul 1770	Charles Town	Z	27-33
Moubray, Lillias	24 May 1765		W	257-258
Moultrie, John			&	15-16
Mouncey, John	-- Sep 1762	Charles Town	V	306-309
Mountgomery, Samuel	7 Jun 1751		R(1)	24
Mouzon, Henry	5 May 1750		B	237
Mouzon, Henry Jr.	17 Apr 1777		BB	39
Mouzon, Lewis	7 Feb 1756		R(2)	426-428
Mouzon, Lewis	23 Mar 1774	St. James Parish, Santee	&	339
Mouzon, Lewis Jr	16 Feb 1748/9		B	50-52
Muckleroy, Agnes	25 Sep 1760		T	414
Muirhead, Alexander	19 Jun 1767		W	446
Mull, John			S	104
Mullins, John	10 Jun 1755		R(2)	348-349
[Mullins,] William	22 Jul 1777		CC	253
Muncrieff, John			B	101-103
Munk, George	4 Apr 1765		W	250-251
Munk, Timothy			W	104-105
Munrow, Daniel			W	287-288

Name	Date	Location	Vol. & pages	
Murcheson, Roderick	27 Nov 1780		BB	170-171
Murphy, Archibald	18 Mar 1768		X	360
Murphy, Hugh	19 Sep 1766		W	321-322
Murphy, Josiah	31 Dec 1771		Z	149-150
Murphy, Dr. Mathew	21 Dec 1776	Colleton Co.	BB	20
Murphy, Michael	10 Apr 1758		S	356-357
Murphy, Michael	16 Dec 1777		CC	287-288
Murphy, Moses	2 Oct 1758		T	86
Murphy, Thomas		Uhaws	R(2)	245-246
Murray, Alexander	11 Feb 1746/7	Charles Town	MM	71-73
Murray, Alex'r	4 Feb 1773		&	277-278
Murray, Alexander	28 Jan 1782	Union Street [Charlestown]	BB	251-254
Murray, Joseph	22 May 1754	Santee	R(2)	208-209
Murray, Joseph	15 Feb 1762		V	107-108
Murray, Rev. Thomas	1 Nov 1753	John's Island	R(2)	73-74
Murray, William	15 Jul 1768	St. Bartholomews Parish, Colleton Co.	X	360-361
Murrell, Francis	23 Sep 1754	St. Johns, Berkley	R(2)	310-311
Murrell, John	12 Feb 1760		T	296
Murrell, Mrs. Susanna	29 Jun 1773		&	276-277
Murriele, Robt Sr.	16 Mar 1762		V	151-153
Murry, John	Mar 1774		&	548-549
Murry, Martha	-- Aug 1747		MM	155-156
Mursett, Peter	30 Jan 1781		B	169
Myers, John			&	51-52
Myers, John			Z	122-123
Nagel, Hands		? Windsor	CC	208-209
Nail, Daniel			&	206-209
Nailor, William Rigby	26 Oct 1773	Charles Town	Z	416-417
Napier, John	18 Mar 1769		Y	88
Nash, Sam	26 Aug 1767		Y	8
Naylor, John	16 Feb 1747/8		MM	267-269
Neel, Andrew	18 Mar 1777		CC	285-286
Neil, Sarah widow	30 Aug 1756	James Island	R(2)	555-557
Neill, Archd.	26 Feb 1754		R(2)	169-171
Neilson, Jared			R(2)	412
Neilson, Jared Jr.	22 Dec 1772		Z	291
Neilson, John			T	205-206
Neilson, John			&	419
Neilson, Mathew	2 Jul 1771	St. Marks Parish, Craven County	Z	54-55
Neilson, Samuel	22 Jul 1767		X	118-119
[Neilson, Thomas]	22 Dec 1772	St. Marks Parish	Z	290
Neilson, William	6 & 7 Sep 1757		S	211-214
Neilson, William	20 Mar 1772		&	52
Nelme, William	2 Apr 1752	Charles Town	R(1)	346-347
Nelson, Ann			W	63-64
Nelson, Jannet			AA	111
Nelson, Margaret	30 Dec 1772		Z	292
Nesmith, John Jr.	21 Feb 1749/50		B	225
Nesmith, Robt	2 Sep 1769		Y	123-124
Newman, Deliverance	19 Apr 1759		T	177
Newman, Edward	6 Nov 1764	Charlestown	W	157-159
Newman, Edward	31 Jan 1772		&	191
Newman, James			T	441-442
Newman, Robert	11 Nov 1747		MM	209-210
Newman, Robert	18 Mar 1762		V	190-191
Newman, Samuel	2 May 1758		S	394-397
Newman, Samuel	29 May 1771		Y	460-462
Newman, Thomas	3 Mar 1756		R(2)	453-454
Newman, Thomas			&	34-35
Newton, Benjamin	10 May 1764		W	64
Newton, Isaac	29 Jun 1768		X	350b
Neyle, John	20 Dec 1767	Charles Town	X	320-321
Nicholes, Joseph			V	63-64
Nicholes, Stephen	14 Jun 1759		T	222
Nichols, Isaac	12 & 14 Jun 1759		T	206-210

Name	Date	Location	Vol. & pages
Nichols, Isaac	4 Mar 1768		X 316-320
Nichols, Isaac	24 Nov 1773	St. Pauls Parish	Z 432-434
Nichols, Isaac	22 Jun 1774		& 420-421
Nichols, Elizabeth	10 Dec 1755		R(2) 393
Nichols, Samuel	13 Jun 1755		R(2) 339-340
Nichols, Thomas Junr	16 Jun 1767		X 76-77
Nicholson, Francis	12 Jan 1778		CC 405
Nicholson, John	17 Mar 1752		R(1) 344-345
Nickman, Isaac	14 May 1756	Craven Co.	R(2) 506
Nicles, Margaret	5 Oct 1770		Y 447
Nielson, William Junr	16 Aug 1766	Black River	W 308
Nightingale, Thos	13 Nov 1769		Y 218-220
Nilson, Janet			& 563
Nisbett, Alexander	26 Feb 1754		R(2) 164-167
Nisbett, Alexander			& 369-370
Nivie, James	11 Jul 1767		X 81-82
Nix, Edward	5 Jun 1777		AA 229-230
Nicholls, Isaac	20 Dec 1776	St. Pauls Parish	AA 185-186
Nicholls, Samuel	4 Feb 1777	St. Bartholomews Parish, Coleton Co.	AA 182-183
Nisbett, John Baronet	17 Mar 1777	St. Johns Parish	BB 49-52
Norman, Barah	30 Jan 1771		Y 380
Norman, George	1 Jul 1772		Z 237-239
Norman, John	20 Jan 1758		S 282-285
Norman, John	25 Apr 1764		W 90-91
Norman, Joseph	22 May 1747	Goose Creek	MM 104-106
Norman, Joseph	18 Jan 1765		W 215-216
Norman, Mary	29 Sep 1750		T 129
Normand, Philip	10 Dec 1756	St. James Santee Parish	S 28-29
Norris, Charles			Z 148-149
Norris, Robert	15 Apr 1769	Long Cane Settlement, Granville Co.	X 450-452
[North, Edward]			M 290-292
North, Edwd Jr.			B 103-105
North, Edwd Jr.	30 Sep 1749		B 165-166
North, Capt. John		St. Bartholomews Parish	W 271-373
North, Richd.	16 Mar 1774	Edisto River(?)	& 449-451
Norton, Gideon	14 Apr 1762		V 209-213
Norton, Hanaway	31 Oct 1749		B 183-184
Norton, Hanway			T 30
Norton, John	9 Sep 1774		AA 16-17
Norton, Kenaway	21 Oct 1777		CC 257
Norvell, James	26 Feb 1771	St. Marks Parish, Craven County	Y 417
Nuffer, Herman	17 Jun 1777	Charles Town	BB 67
Nugent, Robert	18 Aug 1770		Y 334-335
Nutt, James			W 328
Nygh, Dr. Peter	10 Dec 1756	Charles Town	S 1; 8
Oatham, Thomas			T 399
Oats, Edward	10 May 1781	Charlestown	BB 183-185
Obrian, Morgan			W 19
O Brien, James			Y 440-443
Odom, Isaac	9 Oct 1767		X 271-272
Ogier, Lewis	24 Apr 1781		BB 151-152
O Hair, John	23 Dec 1776	Purrysburgh, St. Peters 'Parish	AA 178-179
O heir, John	1 Jul 1777		AA 219
Ohlen, John	2 Feb 1769		X 420
Oldfield, Thomas	24 Mar 1759		T 171-172
Oldham, Benet	14 Nov 1768	Charles Town	X 407
Oliver, John	25 Nov 1768		X 375
Oliver, Margaret			W 243-244
Oliver, Mark	12 Mar 1752	Christ Church Parish	R(1) 369-370
Oliver, Peter	9 Apr 1755		R(2) 323
Oliver, Robert	19 Jan 1759		T 105
Oliveros, Jacob			R(1) 409-410
ONeal, Charles	26 Jun 1770		Y 280-281

Name	Date	Location	Vol. & pages	
Oneal, Frederick	18 Mar 1768		X	289-291
Oneal, Capt. Henry	3 Sep 1761		V	69
Opry, Richard	7 Apr 1767		W	417
Oram, Joseph	28 Aug 1769		Y	147
Orford, John	22 Feb 1769		Y	38
Ormsbee, Shuball	11 Mar 1769		X	443-444
Orr, Rev.	30 May 1757		S	139-140
Orr, James	27 Sep 1770		Y	321-322
Orr, Mary	27 Sep 1770		Y	321
Orr, Robert			B	393
Osborne, Joseph	6 Feb 1775		&	525
Osborn, Willm	18 May 1762		V	202
Oswald, James	2 Apr 1777		BB	65
Oswald, Joseph			CC	128-131
Oswald, Robert Senr.	21 Dec 1762		V	351-354
Oswald, William	2 Oct 1764		V	275-276
Oswell, Joseph	30 Jun 1749	Ponpon	B	132
Ott, John	5 Feb 1773	Tugudoo, near Will town	&	176-177
Ott, John	16 Mar 1772		&	36-37
Ott, Martin	28 Oct 1774		&	474
Otterson, James	19 Apr 1768		X	359
Ouldfield, John	15 Mar 1753		R(1)	527-530
Ousley, James	21 May 1757		S	137-138
Ousley, James	27 Aug 1762	Christ Church Parish	V	292
Owen, John	21 Jul 1752	Charles Town	R(1)	432-425
Owen, John	5 Sep 1750		B	343
Owens, James			W	309-310
Oxton, John	31 Oct 1761		V	84
Oyston, John	8 Jan 1763	Charlestown	V	342-343
Pachelbel, Charles Theodore	11 Oct		R(1)	34
Pacy, Thomas			Y	281-282
[Padgett, William]	27 Nov 1769		Y	160
Page, John	25 Nov 1768	St. Bartholomews Parish, Colleton Co.	X	399-400
Page, Mrs. Sarah	4 Mar 1755		R(2)	339
Page, William	8 Jul 1773		&	279-280
Pagett, John	1747/8		MM	281-285
Pagett, Frances widow	18 Dec 1746		MM	49-50
Pagett, Henry	17 Jul 1767	River May	X	167-172
Pagett, Thomas	31 May 1774		&	367
Paisley, Robert	14 Apr 1761		T	537-538
Palmenter, William	10 Nov 1772		Z	290
Palmer, Mrs. Ann	26 Feb 1771	Prince Williams Parish	Y	464
Palmer, Edmund	20 Jan 1752		R(1)	165-166
Palmer, Elizabeth	28 Sep 1761		V	58
Palmer, Evans	26 Jan 1753		R(1)	533-534
Palmer, Henry	5 Sep 1771		Z	113-114
Palmer, John	27 Mar 1761	Chas. Town	T	507
Palmer, John	28 Nov 1774	St. Helena Parish	&	477-480
Palmer, Thomas	19 Jan 1749/50	Christ Church Parish	B	219
Palmer, Thomas	17 May 1750		B	274
Palmer, Maj. William	25 Jun 1754		R(2)	222-224
Panting, Revd. Thomas	28 Sep 1771	St. Andrews Parish	Z	139-143
Paris, Alexander			R(1)	451-453
Parker, William	20 Oct 1752	Prince Williams Parish, Granville Co.	R(1)	457
Parkinson, Thomas	11 Jul 1765		W	277-278
Parmenter, Benjamin	13 Nov 1772	Hilton Head	&	166-168
Parmenter, Benjamin Jr.	3 Apr 1773	Hilton head	Z	351-353
Parmenter, John	2 Sep 1776	Hilton Head	&	609
Parmenter, John	2 Sep 1776		CC	34-35
Parmenter, Joseph	26 Mar 1764	Wilton Head	W	123-125
Parmenter, Joseph	9 May 1768		X	353-354
Parmenter, Joseph	14 May 1773		&	248-249
Parmenter, Thomas	29 Jan 1750/1		B	417-418
Parmenter, Thomas	22 Sep 1769		Y	133-134
Parnham, John	24 Aug 1774	Charles Town	&	461

Name	Date	Location	Vol. & pages	
Parrot, Hannah	4 Oct 1762		V	276
Parson, William	2 May 1750	Craven Co.	R(1)	53-54
Parsons, James	9 Nov 1779	Charles Town	BB	190-201
Partridge, Ann	11 Nov 1758		T	99-100
Pasco, Michael	7 Jul 1755		R(2)	360
[Paterson, William]	3 May 1771		Y	434-435
Patient, John		Charles Town	V	54-55
Patrick, Luke	14 Dec 1771	Colleton Co.	Z	143
Patrick, Luke	20 Aug 1771	St. Georges	Z	85-86
Patrick, Luke	12 Aug 1775	St. Bartholomews Parish	AA	116
Patrick, Robert Sr.	29 Nov 1777		CC	312
Patterson, John			V	47-48
Patterson, John	18 Mar 1777		AA	212
Patterson, Robt	23 Apr 1770	Wadmalaw	Y	273-275
Pattison, John			BB	243
Patton, Arthur	24 Jan 1772	Granville Co.	Z	197-199
Patton, James	29 Mar 1767		W	424-425
Paul, Abraham			R(2)	284
Paul, Peter	28 Nov 1768		X	404
Paul Cordes, James			BB	17
Pawley, George	15 Feb 1774		&	331-333
Pawley, Percifl.	16 May 1752		V	348-351
Pawley, Robert	23 Dec 1762		V	331-335
Pawley, Shory	2 Jul 1777	Waccamaw, Prince Georges Parish	AA	223-226
Pawley, William	2 Apr 1777	Waccamaw, Prince Georges Parish, Draven Co.	AA	215-218
Pawly, Mary Elizath.	8 Dec 1770		Y	396
Paxton, James	14 Jun 1753		R(2)	45
Payne, Ephraim	26 Mar 1763	St. Bartholomews Parish	V	363-364
Payne, Nathaniel	7 Apr 1767		W	434-435
Payton, Benjamin	27 Sep 1769		Y	186-187
Peacock, Ann	16 Jan 1769	Charles Town	X	409-410
Peacom, John	8 & 9 Dec 1752		R(1)	486-489
Peak, Stephen	18 Feb 1767		W	407-408
Peak, William	9 Mar 1762	Prince Georges Parish	X	435-438
Pearce, John	9 Aug 1758		T	62
Pearce, John	25 Jan 1765		W	407
Pearis, Capt. Robert	4 Mar 1782		BB	251
Peire, Rene	26 Jul 1766		X	51-54
Pellams, Dr. William	18 Jan 1768		X	273-277
Pelot, John	27 Jul 1776		&	619-620
Pelot, Jonas	29 Nov 1768		X	402
Pelott, Rev. Francis	20 Jan 1776		AA	80-82
Pendall, Richard			X	46
Pender, Capt. George	23 Jul 1767		X	181
Pender, Paul	10 May 1770		Y	237-238
Pendergrass, Darby	11 Sep 1780	Charles Town	BB	86
Pendly, Thomas			V	336
[Penington], Abraham	11 Oct 1756		S	6
Pennabit, John Peter			R(1)	365
Pennington, Isaac	8 Jan 1762		T	432-433
Pennington, Jacob	3 Dec 1774		AA	41-42
Pennington, Jacob	18 Mar 1777		AA	231-232
Pennington, Mary	28 Oct 1762		V	289-290
Penny, Jno.	25 Nov 1767		X	218
Penny, William	21 Dec 1774	Round O	AA	68-69
Pepper, Daniel	2 Jan 1771		Y	421-422
Pepper, Gilbert	19 Dec 1766		W	366-368
Perdriau, Benjamin	23 Apr 1764		W	99
Perdriau, John	23 Aug 1771		Z	83-84
Perkins, John		Prince Williams Parish	CC	345-346
Perkins, Rees	16 Nov 1767		X	218-219
Perkins, Samuel	18 May 1764		W	131-133
Perkins, Mrs. Sarah	29 Mar 1773		Z	313-315
Perkis, Mrs. Mary			Z	372
Peronneau, Alexander Jr.	14 Dec 1773		Z	430-431
Peronneau, Alex'd Senr		Charles Town	&	396-399

Name	Date	Location	Vol. & pages
Peronneau, Aurthor	23 Dec 1774	Charles town	AA 36
Peronneau, Henry	20 Jul 1754		R(2) 159-162
Peronneau, Samuel	10 Mar 1756	Charles Town	R(2) 416-424
Peronneau, Samuel	17 Nov 1768	Charlestown	X 430-431
Perrenneau, James	4 Dec 1777	Charles town	CC 390-392
Perrett, John Senr	14 Jul 1777		CC 210-213
Perriman, James	25 May 1754		R(2) 188-189
Perriman, James	26 Mar 1764		W 88-89
Perriman, William			B 2-3
Perronneau, Elizabeth widow	29 Sept 1767	Charles Town	Y 2-3
Perry, Becca		St. Pauls Parish	S 208
Perry, Benjamin	11 Mar 1762		V 115-117
Perry, Edward	16 Apr 1773		Z 408-409
Perry, Edward Sr.	29 Sep 1755		R(2) 377
Perry, Edward Senr	16 May 1771		Z 34-38
Perry, Francis	1 Apr 1767	Charles Town	W 430-431
Parry, Joseph	7 Sep 1756		R(2) 535
Perry, Joseph	20 May 1771	St. Bartholomews Parish	Z 19-20
Perry, Josiah	14 Oct 1773	St. Pauls Parish	Z 417-421
Perry, Peter	14 Nov 1765		X 189-191
Perry, Mrs. Rosamond widow	30 Apr 1773		Z 406-408
Perry, William	5 Jun 1759		T 224
Peter [free Negro?]	6 Sep 1764		W 260
Peter, Jacob	14 May 1759		T 225
Peter, John			B 202-203
Peter, John	4 Jan 1752		R(1) 290-293
Peter, John	12 Aug 1752		R(1) 431
Peter, John	3 Jul 1777		CC 246-248
Peter, Mrs. Tabitha	10 Mar 1752		R(1) 366-367
Peters, John	21 Aug 1758		T 39
Peters, John	21 Feb 1754		R(2) 150-151
Peters, Matthias	4 Jul 1770	Jacksonburgh	Y 283
Petit, Wm.			R(2) 355
Petrie, Alexander	28 Jul 1768	Charles Town	X 365-369
Petty, Henry	16 Dec 1748		B 54-75
Peyn, Doctor Jacobus	9 Dec 1756		S 17-18
Peyre, E. W. Rene			& 452-454
Peyre, Judith	20 Feb 1758		S 359
Peyre, Phillip	7 Aug 1746	Craven Co., St. James Parish Santee	MM 27-30
Peyre, Samuel	18 Oct 1761		T 83-86
Peyre, Mrs. Sarah			& 75-76
Phelps, Thomas	15 Feb 1778		CC 401
Phenny, John	6 May 1754		R(2) 200-201
Philips, James	22 Jun 1773	Charles Town	Z 385
Philips, Thomas			V 72-73
Phillips & Humphrys	4 Sep 1777		CC 387-389
Phillips, Susanah	25 Aug 1747	Charles Town	B 86-87
[Philp], George	11 Mar 1747		MM 272-273
Phipps, John	17 Oct 1746		MM 33-37
Phipps, Joseph	31 Aug 1769		Y 113-113
Pickering, Joseph		Charles Town	T 246-250
Pickham, William	10 Oct 1754		R(2) 271
Pierce, Rev. James	10 Feb 1772	Beaufort	& 11-12
Pilkington, Gabriel	2 May 1764		W 66
Pillams, Mary	11 May 1769	St. Bartholomews Parish, Colleton Co.	X 464-466
Pimenta, Leah	14 Oct 1768		Y 68-69
Pimento, Moses			W 149-153
Pinckney, Roger	8 & 9 Nov 1776		& 633-641
Pinckney, Lt. Thomas	17 Jul 1770	St. Bartholomews Parish	Y 307-309
Pinney, John	16 Jun 1756		R(2) 474-475
Pitcock, Lewis	14 Jan 1771	George Town	Y 409-411
Player, Joseph	21 Aug 1777		CC 370
Player, Thos.	4 Aug 1774		AA 20a-21
Plowden, Edward	25 Jul 1763		V 497-498

Name	Date	Location	Vol. & pages	
Plowman, Elizabeth widow	31 Jan 1772		Z	203-204
Plowman, Jacob			Y	159-160
Poinsett, Elisha Sr.	10 Apr 1771	Charles Town	Z	21-22
Pollard, Den.			BB	268
Poole, Mrs. Elizabeth			S	421-423
Poole, Joseph	1759		T	259-262
Poole, Thomas	19 Jun 1754	Chars. Town	R(2)	233-235
Poole, Thomas	29 May 1769		Y	46
Poole, William	19 Apr 1750		B	289-290
Poor, Patrick	9 Dec 1749		B	201-202
Pope, James	30 Oct 1770		Y	342-343
Porcher, Joseph	17 Apr 1770		Y	230-233
Porcher, Peter	2 Jan 1754		R(2)	101-107
Porcher, Rachel	25 Jan 1748/9		B	54
Port, Thos	4 Apr 1777		BB	58-59
Porter, John	26 Mar 1751		B	409
Porter, John	11 Mar 1768		X	284-285
Porter, Mrs. Sarah	6 May 1767		X	82
Porter, Capt. Thomas	12 Dec 1755	St. Pauls Parish	R(2)	402-403
Porter, William		Christ Church Parish	B	263-264
Postel, Mrs. Judith	27 Oct 1764	Dorchester	W	122-123
Postell, Benj.	21 Dec 1749	St. Georges Parish	B	218
Postell, Elijah	26 Dec 1774	Dorchester	&	484-491
Postell, James	3 Aug 1773	St. Georges Parish	&	285-292
Postell, Margaret	25 Nov 1752		R(1)	468
Postell, Samuel			S	231-232
Potter, John	21 Nov 1776		CC	99-101
Potts, Thomas Senr.	17 Jul 1764		W	178-179
Pou, Gavin	22 May 1775	Orangeburgh	&	563-567
Pouncey, Anthony	7 Jul 1767	Craven Co.	X	78-81
Pouncey, Anthoney	21 Nov 1770		Z	260-262
Poumcy, Wm	1 Dec 1777		CC	288-290
Powell, Peter	25 Feb 1777		AA	187
Powell, Thomas	28 Nov 1757		S	230-231
Powell, Thomas			T	505-506
Power, William	6 Dec 1757		S	214-219
Powers, Richard	8 Sep 1756	Charles Town	R(2)	529
Powers, William	9 Apr 1746	Wadmalaw Island	MM	4
Poyas, John Lewis	1 Jun 1756	Berkley Co.	R(2)	487-488
Poyatt, John	21 Mar 1761		T	541-543
Prater, Philip	14 Dec 1768		X	259-260
Prentice, John	9 Apr 1753		R(1)	546-549
Pressly, David	Apr 1749		B	96-97
Pressly, William	16 Apr 1751		R(1)	20-21
Previtt, Willm.	17 Aug 1774		AA	27-28
Price, Joseph	24 Jun 1766		W	313-314
Price, Martha	3 Apr 1754	Charles Town	R(2)	152-153
Price, Rice		Charles Town	S	297-301
Price, Wm.	19 May 1750		B	269
Prichard, Charles Jacob	20 Jan 1761		T	437-438
Prigg, John	3 Mar 1777		BB	26
Prince, Mrs. Hannah	15 Apr 1769		X	444-445
Prince, Joseph	12 Oct 1761		V	59
Pringle, Robert	10 Dec 1777	Chs. Town	CC	263-264
Prioleau, Elijah	20 Dec 1769	Charles Town	Y	220-223
Prioleau, Samuel	29 Jun 1752		R(1)	412-419
Prise, Hopkin	11 Jan 1782	Charles Town	BB	244-251
Pritchard, John			R(1)	71-72
Pritchit, Rowland			R(1)	66-67
Pritty, Thomas	27 Apr 1757	Craven Co.	S	142-143
Proctor, Hannah	26 Apr 1765	Waccomaw, Prince Georges Parish	X	27
Prothers, John	21 Feb 1775		&	526
Prothrow, James			X	46
Prue, John	27 Feb 1773	Chas town	&	226-229
Punch, Thomas	6 Oct 1768		Z	171-173
Purky, Henry	1 Jan 1765		W	197

Name	Date	Location	Vol. & pages	
Purses, William	11 Aug 1772-27 Apr 1773		&	303-305
Pury, Chas.	15 Jan 1755	Beaufort, Port Royal	R(2)	279-284
Pyatt, Catharine	13 Jan 1772	Georgetown	&	1-2
Quash, Mrs. Elizabeth	2 Jan 1775		&	532-533
Quash, Robert	30 Apr 1772	St. Thomas & St. Denis	&	109-112
Quick, John Wolfgang	15 Jan 1781	Charles Town	BB	128-129
Quincey, Mrs. Elizabeth			R(2)	263-265
Quinche, Lewis	21 Apr 1764	St. Helena Parish	W	54-55
Race, Benjamin			R(2)	334-335
Rae, Rev. John	11 Apr 1762	Williamsburgh	T	540
Raganos, John			S	190
Ragland, John	10 Apr 1773		Z	350-351
Raiford, Martha	1 Nov 1769	Congarees	Y	146
Raiford, Philip	4 Sep 1761		V	45-46
Raiford, Philip Senr	1 Nov 1769		Y	146
Raiford, William			V	214
Rainey, Johnston	1 Jul 1771	Christ Church Parish	Z	64-65
Rake, Thomas	8 Apr 1762		V	148-150
Rall, John	23 Aug ----	Saludy River	AA	208-210
Ramsay, James	19 Apr 1753		R(2)	40-41
Ramsay, Mrs. Sarah	4 Sep 1762		V	310-313
Ramsey, Benjamin	5 May 1753		R(2)	45-46
Ramsey, John	9 Sep 1775	Ninety Six District	AA	119
Randall, Robert	17 Mar 1773		&	220-222
Randall, Mrs. Sarah	27 Oct 1781		BB	228-229
Randall, William	30 Oct 1755	Charles Town	R(2)	372-373
Rantowle, Alexander	15 Dec 1781	St. Philips Parish	BB	242-243
Rantowle, John			Z	482-484
Rantowles, Mrs.			CC	196-198
Rapaile, Havier			CC	386-387
Rape, Vincent	13 Nov 1760		T	435
Rattray, Helen widow	21 Jan 1777	Charlestown	AA	171-172
Rattray, Helen widow	18 Dec 1776	Chs Town	CC	107-109
Rattray, John	30 Dec 1761		V	99-105
Raven, John Capt.	21 Feb 1765		W	238-241
Raven, William	4 Feb 1769	Charlestown	X	419-420
Raven, Wm.	31 Oct 1765	Charlestown	Y	18-26
Ravenel, Daniel	18 Mar 1775	Charlestown	&	621-622
Ravenel, Daniel Senr		St. Johns, Berkley	&	622-625
Ravenel, James	26 Dec 1779		BB	270-272
Ravenel, Rene Jr.	8 Aug 1750	Berkley Co.	B	344-345
Ravol, Gabriel	16 Mar 1770	St. Peters, Purysburgh	Y	229-230
Rawlins, Robert	4 & 11 Mar 1772		Z	208-209
Ray, James	21 Mar 1754		R(2)	174
Ray, John	6 Aug 1768		X	378-379
Ray, John Junr	8 Jul 1761		V	27-28
Read, John	31 Jul 1766	Beaufort	W	310
Reape, John	9 Dec		X	279-280
Redman, John	27 Jul 1747	Charles Town	MM	138-139
Rees, Evans			T	234-235
Rees, Roger	9 Oct 1762		V	283
Rees, Thomas	2 Dec 1762		V	309
Reeves, Dr. Ambrose	14 Apr 1750	Granville Co.	B	257-258
Reid, George			X	235
Reid, James	8 Dec 1769	Charles Town	Y	204-207
Reid, John	20 Aug 1764		W	167-168
Reid, Patrick	5 Jul 1754	Charles Town	R(2)	229-231
Reid, Robert	11 Apr 1764		W	57-58
Reid, Samuel	27 Mar 1764		W	59-60
Reiley, Barnaby			R(2)	311
Reiley, James			&	422
Reiley, Martha			R(2)	310
[Reily, Barnabè]	7 Apr 1747[?]		MM	279-280
Reily, Bryan[?]	5 Feb 1752		R(1)	282-284
Reily, John			R(2)	316-322
Reily, John			R(2)	331

Name	Date	Location	Vol. & pages	
Rembert, Andrew Jun.			BB	13-14
Rembert, Andrew Senr.			BB	14
Remingsparger, John Jacob	15 Jul 1754		R(2)	236-237
Remington, John	23 Jan 1781		BB	107-108
Reynolds, Elenor	3 Dec 1776		CC	201
Reynolds, Richard	6 Apr 1759		T	169-170
Reynolds, Richard	27 Jan 1768	Granville Co.	X	262
Reynolds, Williams	16 Dec 1756		S	29-30
Rhoda, Mrs. Dorathy	15 Aug 1757		S	180
Rhodus, Joseph	18 Feb 1773		&	244
Rich, Lewis	12 Oct 1769		Y	131
Rich, William	26 Jul 1754		S	55-56
Richards, John	Nov 1747		MM	280
Richardson, Capt. Henry	26 Oct 1768		X	408-409
Richardson, Rev. William	28 Dec 1771		Z	148
Richbourd, Charles			Z	77-78
Richbourg, Samuel	17 Jan 1777		BB	21
Richmond, Henry	18 Mar 1754		R(2)	203
Ridgill, William	31 Oct 1770		Z	40-41
Rife, John	6 Jan 1777		AA	177-178
Rigg, Alexander	16 Dec 1771	Charles Town	Z	139
Riggs, Cap. Thomas	18 Feb 1754		R(2)	110-115
Rippin, Aaron	5 May 1748		MM	313-314
Rippins, Lydia	20 Feb 1753		R(1)	324-325
Rippon, Aaron			S	196-197
Rippon, Christopher	20 Mar 1758		T	43
Rippon, Edward	3 Feb 1758		S	320-324
Rippon, Hannah	4 Sep 1767		X	173-174
Rippon, Martha	3 Jan 1769	Edisto Island	X	423
Rippon, Richard			W	168-170
Rippons, Lydia			R(1)	398-399
Rise[?], Lewis	23 Mar 1750/1		B	409
Ritch, Willm.	28 Jun 1751		R(1)	50
Rivers, Daniel	30 Jun 1764	James Island	W	170-171
Rivers, George	17 Aug 1749		B	176-178
Rivers, Henry	6 Jan 1776		BB	25
Rivers, Isaac	17 Nov 1777	Camden District	CC	284-285
Rivers, John	16 May 1764		W	129
Rivers, John	11 Apr 1769	Wappeo, St. Andrews	X	449
Rivers, Jonathan			W	102-104
Rivers, Joseph	18 Nov 1758		T	86-89
Rivers, Joseph & Elizabeth	7 May 1768		X	332
Rivers, John	7 Jun 1773		&	278-279
Rivers, Joseph	11 Mar 1746/7		MM	103
Rivers, Nehemiah	9 Jul 1770		Y	357
Rivers, Robert	30 Oct 1764	James Island	W	196-197
Rivers, Robert	5 Feb 1774		Z	491
Rivers, William			R(1)	327a-327b
Rivers, William			Z	395-396
Robbins, Daniel		Little River, Prince George Parish, Craven Co.	CC	339-340
Roberson, Ann	18 Jan 1758		S	326
Roberson, Joseph			V	324-325
Robert, Jonah	9 Aug 1777		CC	276-277
Robert, Peter	19 Feb 1767		X	161-162
Roberts, Abraham	12 Mar 1762		V	150-151
Roberts, Benjn.	17 Nov 1753		R(2)	181
Roberts, Charles	29 Jan 1780		BB	92
Roberts, David	28 Mar 1768		X	341-342
Roberts, John	21 & 23 Feb 1760		T	286-289
Roberts, John	2 Sep 1768		X	382
Roberts, Wm.	12 Dec 1770	St. James Parish, Santee	Y	379
Roberts, Doctor William	9 Jun 1777	Charlestown	AA	246-249
Robertson, Adam		St. Bartholomews Parish, Ashepoo	V	361
Robertson, Ann widow	10 Dec 1757	Charles Town; Augusta, Ga.	S	226-229
Robertson, Charles	30 Apr 1770		Y	320

Name	Date	Location	Vol. & pages	
Robertson, James	23 Aug 1748		B	4-10
Robertson, John			R(1)	174
Robertson, Robert	24 Apr 1781	Charlestown	BB	181
Robeson, Robert	2 Jan 1776	Camden Dist.	CC	279-281
Robinson, Alexander Sr.		Little River, Craven Co.	X	216
Robinson, Charles			Y	319
Robinson, Edmund	29 May 1750	Georgetown	B	319
Robinson, Jane	17 May 1755		R(2)	344-345
Robinson, John	28 Aug 1770		Y	320
Robinson, Thomas	30 Dec 1747		MM	247-248
Robinson, Thomas			B	402-403
Robison, William	2 Oct 1773	North Carolina	Z	398-399
Roblin, Peter Senr	18 Sep 1767		Y	11
Roblin, Philip	21 Feb 1771		Y	419
Roch, John George			R(2)	345
Roche, Francis	25 Jan 1768		X	250-252
Roche, Jordan	22 Jun 1752		R(1)	437-440
Roche, Michael	18 Oct 1752		R(1)	462-463
Rockford, James	10 Mar 1762		V	146-147
Rodgers, Capt. James	8 Mar 1762	Charles Town	V	110-111
Rodgers, Capt. James	14 Apr 1769	Charles Town	Y	117-118
Roffe, John	5 Feb 1767		W	383-385
Rogers, Ann	11 May 1773		&	244-245
Rogers, Nicholas	12 Sep 1760		T	381-383
Rogers, Robert	19 Aug 1754		R(2)	158-159
Rogers, [William]	9 Feb 1773		Z	304-305
Rogerson, John	9 Aug ----		V	500-501
Rogerson, John	31 Aug 1768		X	379
Roof, Leonard	12 Mar 1768		X	385
Roro, Michael	29 Sep 1755	Purysburg	T	174
Rosch, Herman	10 May 1773		&	270-271
Rose, Elizabeth	5 Jun 1759		T	199
Rose, Elizabeth	6 Oct 1761		T	254
Rose, Elizabeth & Margt. Lucia	21 Jul 1769		Y	114-115
Rose, Susannah			T	395-396
Rose, Thomas	15 Jun 1756		S	427-431
Rose, William	9 Apr 1756		R(2)	449-450
Rose, Dr. William	20 May 1756	Prince William Parish	R(2)	461-467
Rose, Dr. William	31 Dec 1766		X	22-27
[Ross], Alexander	6 Oct 1777		CC	377
Roth, Jacob	5 May 1768	Orangeburgh	X	349-350
Rothe, Peter			T	399
Rothmahler, Miss Ann	21 Feb 1770	George Town	Y	195
Rouk, John George	17 Apr 1773	Amelia Township	Z	339
Roulain, Daniel	13 Jun 1758		T	24
Roulain, James	1 Feb 1781	St. Thomas & St. Denis Parish	BB	116-117
Rousham, James	13 Feb 1755		R(2)	311-312
Rowand, Robert	14 Mar 1759		T	139b
Rowman, Christian	25 Mar 1763		V	483
Rowser, Richard			T	254
Rowser, William			X	396
Royal, Peter			Y	249-250
Royer, John	4 Jan 1754	Christ Church Parish	R(2)	94-95
Rumph, Abraham			CC	326-329
Rumph, Peter	25 Feb 1762		V	201
Rupp, Francis	14 Jun 1777		AA	226-227
Russ, [Abijah]	13 --- ----		&	415-416
Russ, David	11 Apr ----		T	173-174
Russ, John	22 Jun 1763		V	461-462
Russ, Jonathan	29 Jun 1763		V	458-461
Russal, Jeremiah	11 Sep 1749		B	193-195
Russe, Joseph	13 Aug 1746	Colleton Co., St. Johns Parish	MM	4-8
Russell, Alexander	6 Mar 1771		Z	12-13
Russell, Mrs. Grace	11 Nov 1776		CC	137-140
Russell, James			AA	241-242

Name	Date	Location	Vol. & pages	
Russell, Jeremiah	23 Apr 1752		R(1)	348
Russell, John	29 Dec 1779		BB	99
Russell, Joseph	5 Aug 1761		V	37
Russell, Mary	1 Jul 1754		R(2)	226-227
Russell, Mary	3 Mar ----		R(2)	326
Russell, Mary	22 Feb 1764	St. Thomas' Parish	W	17-18
Russell, Mary	16 Aug 1774		AA	28-29
Russell, Samuel	17 Oct 1757	Craven Co.	S	210-211
Russell, Stephen	18 Jul 1765		X	40
Russell, Walter	10 Jul 1776	Charles Town	CC	9
Russell, William	20 May 1774		AA	57-60
Rutherford, Robt.	8 Sep 1776		CC	109-110
Rutledge, Andrew	11 Dec 1755	Chehaw	R(2)	409-410
Rutledge, Andrew		Charles Town	R(2)	410-412
Rutledge, John	22 Jan 1756	Christ Church Parish	R(2)	408-409
Ryan, Jeremiah	17 Nov 1774	Charlestown	&	499-500
Ryley, John	17 Dec 1767		X	256
Sabb, William	15 Jul 1767	St. Matthews Parish	X	87-88
St. Germain, Lucius			CC	412
St. John, John			R(2)	442
St. John, Miller	1 Apr 1757		S	52-53
St. Ledger, John	20 Sep 1769	Charles Town	Y	127
Sallens, Robert	29 Mar 1757		S	68-70
Salster, Christopher	26 Se- 1768		X	388
Salters, Richard	16 Jul 1773	Euhaws, St. Peters Parish	&	282-284
Samplo, Francis	14 Jul 1752		R(1)	421
Sams, Jos.	19 Feb 1756		R(2)	485-486
Sams, Capt. Robert	19 Dec 1760		T	429-432
Sams, Robert Junr.	7 Nov 1760		T	417-418
Samuels, John and Marian	24 Mar 1762		V	223-225
Samwayes, Hill	18 Spe 1771	Prince Williams Parish	Z	146-147
[Samways, Henry]			W	45-48
Samways, John	19 Nov 1771		Z	154-157
Sanders, Charles	21 Dec 1749		B	216
Sanders, George	27 Nov 1755		R(2)	395
Sanders, James minor	10 Dec 1750		B	352-353
Sanders, Jno.	25 May 1758		S	432-434
Sanders, John Senr.			W	25
Sanders, Joseph	5 Dec 1764	St. Bartholomews Parish	W	190-192
Sanders, Capt. Joshua	4 Sep 1751	Colleton Co.	R(1)	68-71
Sanders, Lawrence	2 May 1751		B	441-443
Sanders, Samuel			R(1)	297-298
Sanders, Wm.	30 Jul 1763		V	474-476
Sanders, Wm.	8 Feb 1777	St. Georges Parish	CC	134-137
Sandiford, James	23 Feb 1761		T	496-497
Sandiford, John	1 May 1750		B	276-277
Sandiford, John	13 Apr 1753		R(2)	36-37
Sandiford, Ralph	18 Feb 1762		V	129-130
Sands, James	24 Aug 1769		Y	132-133
Sandwell, Elianor	4 Dec 1751		R(1)	167-170
Sanks, George	6 May 1772	Charlestown	&	78-79
Saragosa, Francis	14 Sep 1772	Colleton Co.	&	142
Sarrazin, Moreau	4 May 1761		T	578-579
Sarreau, Mary			R(2)	403-404
Satur, Abraham	25 Feb 1747/8	St. James Santee, Craven Co.	MM	261-265
Saunders, Francis	31 Jul 1781		BB	182
Saunders, George	9 May 1772	St. Marks Parish	&	71-72
Saunderson, Alexander	14 Mar 1777		AA	179-180
Saucer, John	5 Jul 1773		Z	363-364
Savage, Benja.	29 Feb 1750	Charles Town	B	335-337
Savage, Daniel	12 May 1762	Hilton Head	V	248-249
Savage, Martha	30 Apr 1761	Charles Town	T	590-597
Savineau, James	21 Aug 1765		X	41-42
Savineau, Jane	25 Sep 1764	George town	X	450
Sawer, Elisha	15 Dec 1780		BB	170
Sawyer, Andrew	16 Nov 1776	Prince Williams Parish	BB	24

Name	Date	Location	Vol. & pages	
Saxby, Sarah	8 Mar 1747/8		MM	304-309
Sayrs, Annanias	13 Jan 1774		Z	507-508
Scarlet, James	25 Oct 1744		MM	196-197
Scharenburg, Peter Jacob	28 Aug 1777		CC	370-371
Schermerhorn, Arnont		St. Philips Parish, Charlestown	CC	413-414
Schermerhorn, Mary	1777		AA	258
Scheurer, Martin	2 Mar 1772	Broad River	&	50-51
Schumbert, Conrad	20 Apr 1774		&	445-446
Schwab, Rev. Ernest	14 Aug 1773		Z	530-532
Schwartzkopff, Dr. Nicholas			Z	256-257
Scot, Jannet	1 Aug 1772	Williams Burgh Township	Z	229
Scott, Archibald	26 Mar 1759		T	160-161
Scott, Elizabeth	4 Jan 1771	Wadmelaw Island	Y	394
Scott, Dr. George	25 May 1769	Johns Island	Y	297-298
Scott, Henrietta	5 Apr 1762		V	157
Scott, James	16 Mar 1750/1		B	399
Scott, John	15 Sep 1752		R(1)	457-458
Scott, John	26 Mar 1771	Craven Co., Williamsburgh	Y	430
Scott, Joseph	13 Mar 1750		B	246-247
Scott, Joseph	2 Apr 1760		T	299-300
Scott, Joseph	4 Jul 1766		W	291
Scott, Nathaniel	13 Nov 1780		BB	112-113
Scott, R.			W	292
Scott, Robert	25 Dec 1759		T	243-246
Scott, Samuel	15 Oct 1771		Z	124-125
Scott, Samuel	4 Dec 1776	Jefferses Creek, Prince Fredericks Parish	BB	9
Scott, Thomas	5 Mar 1767	Craven Co.	X	158-159
Scott, Thomas Guillm.	3 Jul 1766		W	298-299
Scott, William	26 Jul 1753	Charles Town	R(2)	67-72
Scott, William	1 May 1765	Charles Town	W	269-270
Screven, Elisha	6 Oct 1758		T	72-76
Screven, Elisha Junr			T	478-481
Screven, Hannah	26 Mar 1772		&	38-43
Screven, James	20 Sep 1758		T	68-72
Screven, Joshua	6 Mar 1764		W	31-33
Screven, Robert	-- Dec 1759		T	279-280
Screven, Samuel			T	481-482
Screven, William			R(2)	522-526
Screven, William	23 Nov 1760		T	420-423
Screven, William	26 Nov 1766		X	131-132
Scrivenor, John	9 Mar 1775	George Town	AA	120-121
Scurlock, Catherine	13 Jun 1758		T	23-24
Seabrook, John	4 Apr 1750		B	321-326
Seabrook, Mrs. Mary	30 Jan 1753		R(1)	511-512
Seabrook, Mrs. Mary	3 Feb 1753	Craven Co.	R(2)	54-55
Seabrook, Robert	11 Apr 1775		AA	100-102
Sealey, John	16 May 1774		&	401-402
Sealy, Joseph Junr.	22 Nov 1763		V	513-516
Sealy, Michael	1 Apr 1762		V	193
Sealy, William	11 Jun 1774		AA	34-36
Sealy, John			X	246-247
Sealy, Jos.	12 Dec 1750		B	410-411
Sealy, Samuel	4 Apr 1767		X	404-405
Sealy, William	29 Apr 1748		MM	311-312
Searson, Thomas	12 Aug 1777		CC	256-257
Seawright, James	29 Sep 1763		W	1
Seawright, Samuel	16 --- 1767	Beaver Creek	X	120-121
Seaman, George	16 Mar 1769	Charles Town, St. Phillips	Y	69-84
Secare, Peter	16 Dec 1769		Y	169-170
Sellers, Mathias	-- Aug 1772	St. Pauls, Colleton Co.	&	117
Sergeant, Richard			S	181-183
Serie, Andrews	19 Nov 1766	Charles Town	W	340
Serre, Sarah	15 Feb 1749/50		B	226
Sewright, William			T	469-470
Seymour, John	29 Aug 1775		CC	64-67
Shackleford, William	15 Jul 1775	George Town	&	574

Name	Date	Location	Vol. & pages	
Shackelford, William	15 Jul 1775	George Town	&	590-591
Shackleford, William	15 Jul 1775	George Town	CC	62-63
Shannon, John	5 Sep 1774	Charles Town	AA	13
Shannon, Robert	26 Mar 1750		R(1)	65
Sharp, Henry	3 May 1773		Z	356-358
Sharp, James	23 Feb 1770		Y	225-227
Sharples, John	26 Jun 1769		Y	60
Shaw, Capt. Alexander			W	274-275
Shaw, John			CC	364
Shaw, Lt. Lachlan	5 Jun 1762		V	438-441
Shaw, Robert	22 Jun 1767		X	119-120
Shaw, Willm.	15 Jan 1750/1	Colleton Co.	B	378-379
Shecutt, Peter	20 Jun 1768		X	361-362
Shekall, James	6 Dec 1776		CC	378-379
Shepards, William			R(2)	469-471
Shepherd, Francis	10 Jan 1758		S	252
Sheperd, Francis	27 Sep 1774	Charles Town	AA	21
Shepheard, Chas.			MM	319-320
Sheppard, Francis	25 Mar 1751		B	445-447
Sheppard, James	1759		T	191-192
Sheriff, Henry	12 Sep 1751		R(1)	103-105
Sherrof, Alexander	15 Sep 1775		CC	61
Shider, Daniel	26 Jun 1759		T	201-202
Shingleton, Richard	28 Oct 1751	Charles Town	R(1)	105-106
Shirea, Elizabeth	6 Dec 1773	Broad River	&	368-369
Shoemaker, Elizabeth	26 Jan 1767		W	374-376
Shoemaker, Thomas			W	25-26
Short, William	8 Mar 1750/1		B	422
Showers, Goerge			S	326-329
Shram, Conrad	12 Mar 1761		T	478
Shrewsberry, Stephen	18 Jun 1747		MM	133-134
Shuble, Frederick	18 May 1764		W	118-119
Shrubsole, Lt. William	10 Jul 1758		S	436-437
Shuler, Daniel			&	315-316
Shuler, James	4 Oct 1754	Berkley Co.	R(2)	278-279
Shute, John	24 Oct 1760		T	386
Shute, John			X	272-273
Shute, Rebeccah	5 Apr 1749		B	87
Sieustrunk, Henry	7 May 1762	Congrees	V	203-204
Simmons, Anthony	-- Jan 1763	Port Royall Island	V	341
Simmons, Ebenezer	3 Nov 1763	Charles Town	W	3-6
Simmons, Ebenezer		Charles Town	Y	240-242
Simmons, Edward	16 Feb 1776	St. Johns Parish	CC	92-94
Simmons, Edward	17 Feb 1776	Prince George, Winyaw	CC	94-96
Simmons, James	1 Jun 1775	Charles Town	&	567-572
Simmons, Peter	6 Jul 1773		Z	371-372
Simmons, Samuel			W	95-99
Simmons, Capt. Thomas	24 May 1749		B	133-134
Simmons, Vincent	5 Jan 1771		Y	364-365
Simmons, William	1 May 1755		R(2)	331-332
Simms, William	28 Jul 1776		BB	8
Simmons, Wm. Clay	9 Nov 1772	Prince Georges Parish	Z	266
Simons, Benjamin	27 May 1772	St. Thomas Parish, Charlestown	&	118-124
Simons, Benjamin	19 Oct 1776	Charlestown	AA	147-148
Simons, Catherine	3 Jun 1775	Orangeburgh Township	CC	41
Simons, Esther			W	303
Simons, Francis	11 Dec 1771		Z	152-154
Simons, Peter	4 Jan 1748/9	St. Thoams & St. Denis Parish	B	81-82
Simons, Colln. Peter	23 Jun 1777	George town	CC	220-225
Simons, Samuel			T	236-237
Simpson, Andw	23 Sep 1773		Z	410-411
Simpson, Christopher	26 Sep 1769	Charles Town	Y	119-123
Simpson, John	9 Dec 1756		S	4
Simpson, Mrs. Sarah	7 Aug 1780	Charlestown	BB	177-178
Simpson, Wm			CC	288
Simpson, Dr. William			Y	353

Name	Date	Location	Vol. & pages	
Simson, Thomas	14 May 1764		W	119-120
Singelton, Benjamin Jr.	20 Jun 1771		Z	20-21
Singellton, Daniel	8 Jul 1761		V	25-26
Singellton, Ebenezr.	12 Feb 1750/1		B	388-389
Singellton, John	7 Jan 1783	St. Bartholomews Parish	BB	258-261
Singellton, Peter	6 Apr 1764		W	107-109
Singellton, Richard	19 Mar 1764		W	49-52
Singellton, Wm	12 Jan 1746/7		MM	57
Singelton, Daniel	21 May 1763		V	437
Singelton, James	5 Jul 1753		R(2)	79-81
Singelton, Mrs. Mary Ann	14 Jul 1774		&	396
[Singleton], Benjamin	27 Sep 1776	St. James Parish, Goosecreek	AA	183-184
Singleton, Col. Benjamin		Goose Creek; Prince George Winyaw, et al	AA	190-195
Singleton, Jane	23 Apr 1778		BB	148-149
Singleton, Mrs. Rebecca	13 Jun 1774	Goosecreek Parish	&	376-377
Singleton, Samuel	13 Oct 1776	St. Bartholomew Parish	AA	142-144
Singleton, Thomas	3 Sep 1773		&	316-317
Sinkler, Jane	26 Feb 1770		Y	195-197
Sinkler, Peter	13 & 14 Jan 1783		BB	264-267
Sinquefield, Moses	5 Dec 1767		X	238
Sisone, Peter			R(2)	378
Skeen, Thomas			T	364-365
Skend, Rev. George	16 Dec 1766		X	134-135
Skene, John	13 Jun 1768		X	355-356
Skinner, Hon. Charles	10 May 1768		X	336-341
Skinner, George	12 Sep 1768		X	389-390
Skrene, Jonathan	Nov 1747		MM	205-206
Slam, Andrew	1 Sep 1755	St. Georges Parish	R(2)	393-394
Slann, Thomas	16 Dec 1770		Y	201-203
Slapfer, Conrad	7 Jun 1777		AA	230
Sleigh, Hugh	31 May 1775		AA	111-114
Sleigh, Hugh	29 Apr 1777		BB	46-47
Sleigh, Samuel Junr.	25 Apr 1764		W	52
Sleigh, Saml Junr	6 May 1773		Z	356
Sleigh, Samuel Senr	28 Feb 1767		W	382-383
Slydensher, Jacob	-- May 1759		T	266
Small, William	30 Jan 175-		R(2)	327
Smart, William		George [Town?]	MM	115-116
Smelie, Susannah	24 Feb 1753		R(1)	516-517
Smilie, Edward	11 Feb 1771		Y	415-417
Smilie, John	3 Jul 1750		B	286-287
Smilie, William	8 May 1755		R(2)	336-337
Smily, James	22 Dec 1777		CC	315-316
Smith, Alexander	25 May 1773	St. Helena Parish	&	260-261
Smith, Archar	19 Apr 1769		Y	44-45
Smith, Aron	29 May 1777	Ninety Six District	CC	184-185
Smith, Barnard	1 Jun 1774	St. Mathews Parish	&	369
Smith, Benjamin	30 Jan 1761		T	524
Smith, Benjamin	7 Jan 1771	Charles Town	Y	369-377
Smith, Miss Charlotte	8 Sep 1777		CC	238
Smith, Christopher	6 Nov 1746		MM	50-51
Smith, Daniel	10 Jun 1752	Charles Town	R(1)	386-387
Smith, Edward	22 May 1756	Charles Town	R(2)	457-458
Smith, Edward			T	522-523
Smith, Elizabeth		Charles Town	B	339-340
Smith, Elizabeth	17 Jul 1751		R(1)	64
Smith, Eliz	17 Jun 1774		&	391
Smith, James	13 Dec 1749		B	216-217
Smith, John	17 Jul 1747		MM	136-137
Smith, John	10 Jul 1765		W	277
Smith, John	4 Mar 1767		W	377-378
Smith, John	28 Nov 1765		X	194
Smith, John	20 Jun 1773		Z	373-374
Smith, John	13 Feb 1782	George Town	BB	244
Smith, Col. John	28 Nov 1753		R(2)	84-87
Smith, Joseph	29 May 1765		W	255

Name	Date	Location	Vol. & pages	
Smith, Joseph	Jan 1781		BB	103-104
Smith, Mrs. Mary widow	15 Apr 1743		R(2)	285-286
Smith, Mary			R(2)	415-416
Smith, Mrs. Mary	25 Jun 1777		AA	227-229
Smith, Mrs. Mary	5 Oct 1776	St. James Parish, Goose Creek	BB	20
Smith, Michael	28 Dec 1776	Beaufort	AA	250
Smith, Nath	19 May 1757		S	131-132
Smith, Puss	5 Dec 1777		CC	312-313
Smith, Robert	27 Feb 1767		X	146-147
Smith, Samuel			R(2)	442
Smith, Samuel		Charles Town	R(2)	456-457
Smith, Samuel	21 Aug 1754	Charles Town	R(2)	167-168
Smith, Samuel	11 Jun 1758		S	417-418
Smith, Samuel	22 Aug 1758		S	419-420
Smith, Sarah	23 Mar 1763		V	368-369
Smith, Stephen	24 Apr 1773		&	232
Smith, Thomas	12 Jan 1763	Berkley Co.	V	355-356
Smith, Thos	22 Feb 1772	St. Helena Parish	&	25-26
Smith, Thomas	9 Aug 1777		CC	276
Smith, Thomas Senr.	27 Sep 1769	Charles Town	Y	167-168
Smith, Thomas Loughton	28 Jul 1773		Z	368-371
Smith, Thomas Rigdon	23 May 1757		S	145-148
Smith, Walter	7 Aug 1769		Y	101-102
Smith, William	1 Nov 1755		R(2)	390
Smith, William	13 Jul 1769		Y	96-100
SmithPeter, John George	7 Nov 1761		V	71-72
Smyth, James	31 Dec 1764	St. Helena Parish	W	225-228
Snell, Henry	6 May 1763		V	376
Snelling, Abram	3 Dec 1750		B	382-384
Snelling, Henry	4 Oct 1756		S	6
Snelling, John	15 Mar 1770	Charles Town	Y	212-214
Snipes, Elizabeth	1 May 1765	St. Pauls Parish	X	203-205
Snither, Jacob	23 Sep 1763		V	542
Snooke, Dr. Cidonious	15 Jul 1766		W	312-313
Snow, John	22 Feb 1751/2		R(1)	327b-328b
Snow, Nathaniel	11 Jan 1750/1		B	361-364
Snow, Nathaniel	31 Mar 1761		T	551-553
Snow, Susannah	30 Mar 1767		W	438
Snow, Susannah			Y	235-236
Sommers, George		St. Pauls Parish	CC	225-229
Sommers, Mrs. Henrietta	16 Sep 1780	Charles Town	BB	157-159
Sooter, James	15 Mar 1755		R(2)	368
Sparrow, Henry	18 Jul 1768		X	406
Spellings, William	1 Mar 1769		X	434-435
Spencer, Francis	7 Jul 1758		T	33
Spencer, Rev. George	18 Oct 1769		Y	138-139
Spencer, John	9 Mar 1761		T	579-581
Spencer, Joseph	19 Jul 1746		MM	48-49
Spencer, Joseph			Y	203-204
Spencer, Oliver	19 Sep 1771		Z	136-137
Spencer, Oliver Sear	24 Jul 1750		B	293-294
Spencer, Sarah widow	20 Feb 1756	John's Island	R(2)	456
Spencer, Thos	18 Jun 1773		Z	382-384
[Spencer, William Jr.]	1 Dec 1774		AA	40
Spencer, William Sr.	17 Apr 1751	James Island	R(1)	298-302
Spens, Doctor David	19 Apr 1754	Stono	R(2)	215-217
Spidle, John	14 Jan 1772		&	1
Spight, Isaac	22 Jul 1775		&	563
Spines, Mrs.			BB	95
Spinior, John			BB	128
Spinks, Thomas	27 Mar 1762		V	265
Splatt, Benja.			V	262-264
Splatt, Benjamin	16 Sep 1767	Granville Co.	Y	3-4
Splatt, John	24 Apr 1750	St. Pauls Parish	B	250
Splatt, John	12 Jan 1753		R(1)	510
Spoade, Mary widow	7 May 1767	Granville Co., St. Helena Parish	X	122

Name	Date	Location	Vol. & pages	
Spoade, William		St. Helena Parish, Granville Co.	W	412-414
Spooler, Philip	17 Apr 1765	St. Pauls Parish	X	31-32
Spooler, Philip		St. Pauls Parish	BB	129
Spraggins, Thos			Z	239-240
Spraggins, Thomas	12 Sep 1772		Z	262-263
Spry, Henry	25 Feb 1771		Y	457-458
Spry, Joseph	9 Sep 1767		X	89-92
Spry, Royal	5 Jun 1747		MM	106-112
Spry, Royal	16 May 1764		W	99-101
Spry, Royal	31 Dec 1770	St. Mark's Parish	Y	366-367
Spry, Samuel	24 Nov 1762	St. Pauls Parish, Colleton County	V	301-305
Spyinger, Samuel	14 Jan 1774	Congarees	Z	452-453
[Stanbridge, William]	10 Feb 1777		BB	24
Stanyarne, Archibald	15 Oct 1773	Charles Town	Z	426-430
Stanyarne, Benjamin	25 Mar 1760		T	411
Stanyarne, Benjamin			R(1)	469-471
Stanyarne, Jehu	5 Mar 1746/7		MM	73-74
Stanyarne, John	8 Mar 1764		W	28-29
Stanyarne, John	1 Jan 1773		Z	305-311
Stanyarne, John (son of John)	8 Mar 1762	Johns Island	V	178-179
Stanyarne, Joseph Senr.	23 Aug 1772	John's Island	&	250-252
Stanyarne, Mrs. Mary	2 Dec 1780	St. Pauls Parish	BB	168-169
Stanyarne[?], Rivers	6 Mar 1755		R(2)	307-308
Stanyarne, Sarah	5 May 1759		T	222-224
Stanyarne, William Jr.	17 Jun 1766		W	302-303
Staph, Margaret	21 Dec 1776	Prince Williams Parish	BB	25
Staples, Abraham	17 May 1750		B	264-265
Starling, John	11 Jul 1774	Charles Town	&	400
Starling, Mary	14 Jan 1765		W	196
Starling, Mary	20 Jan 1770	James Island	Y	200-201
Starrat, Archibald	10 Dec 1767		X	237-239
Starrat, George	10 Apr 1761		T	575-578
Stead, Benjamin	2 Aug 1777	London	CC	217-219
Steal, Robert	-- Mar 1747/8		MM	274-275
Steck, Anthoney	15 Dec 1762		V	319-320
Stedman, Robert	21 Dec 1766	Charles Town	W	353
Steel, Dr. James			T	301-302
Steel, John	10 Oct 1754		R(2)	271
Stent, Daniel	8 Feb 1759		T	172-173
Stephenson, James		Camden District	CC	175-176
Steut, Daniel	5 Sep 1767		X	174
Sterling, John	13 Dec 1749		B	213-214
Stevens, Mrs. Ann	24 Jul 1753		R(2)	53-54
Stevens, Benjamin	14 Feb 1771		Y	438-439
Stevens, David	28 Jan 1763		V	356-359
Stevens, Elizabeth	26 Oct 1771		Z	123-124
Stevens, Jacob Junr.	28 Feb 1774		&	340-341
Stevens, Mrs. Jennet	2 Apr 1752		R(1)	338-339
Stevens, Joseph	16 Dec 1747		MM	259-260
Stevens, Joseph	29 Dec 1760		T	435
Stevens, Margaret	20 Feb 1750/1	Port Royal, Granville Co.	B	392-393
Stevens, Richard	8 Jun 1749	Port Royal, Granville Co.	B	135-136
Stevens, Richard	20 Apr 1767	St. Helena Parish	W	409-411
Stevens, Robert	13 Dec 1752	St. Pauls Parish	R(1)	489-491
Stevens, Samuel	26 Sep 1752		R(1)	450
Stevens, Dr. Samuel	10 Jul ----		T	349-352
Stevens, Mrs. Sarah	17 Mar 1772		&	24-25
Stevens, Thomas	9 Apr 1754		R(2)	156-157
Stevenson, Peter	15 Nov 1776	Amelia Township, St. Mathews Parish, Orangeburgh	AA	233-237
Stewart, Adam	23 Sep 1767		X	174-175
Stewart, Alexander	5 Nov 1763		V	548-550
Stewart, Alexr.	2 Apr 1764		W	58-59
Stewart, Daniel			S	345-347
Stewart, Elizabeth		Williamsburgh, Craven Co.	W	368

Name	Date	Location	Vol. & pages	
Stewart, Elizabeth			CC	235
Stewart, Mrs. Hannah	13 Jan 1781		BB	118
Stewart, John	11 Sep 1747[?]		B	97-98
Stewart, Mrs. Marion	12 Aug 1763		V	550-552
Stewart, Mary	8 Jan 1750/1	Berkley Co.	B	386-387
Stewart, Robt.	21 Nov 1776		CC	105-107
Stewart, William	30 May 1770	Prince Fredericks Parish	Y	283-284
Stiles, Mrs. Ann	9 Oct 1772		&	300-301
Stiles, Ann Garden	29 Aug 1767		X	121
Stiles, Benja.	24 May 1751		R(1)	37-40
Stiles, Benjamin	11 Apr 1753		R(2)	34-36
Stiles, Rebecca	19 Dec 1749		B	207-208
Stoaks, Thomas	24 Feb 1746/7	Ashley ferry	MM	91-92
Stobo, James	12 Mar 1781		BB	214-217
Stobo, Samuel	4 Mar 1762		V	130-131
Stock[?], Anna	12 Apr 1750	Saxagotha Township	B	244
Stock, Gabriel Luickly	-- Mar 1772	St. Bartholomew Parish, Colleton Co.	&	43-45
Stock, Mrs. Rachael		St. Bartholomews Parish, Colleton Co.	&	507-508
Stocks, George	2 Dec 1759	Johns Island	T	272-273
Stocks, Samuel	10 Jul 1753		R(2)	46
Stocks, Thomas	14 Apr 1760		T	303-304
Stoddard, David	10 Feb 1770	Charlestown	Y	187-190
Stoechen, Bodo William	13 Jan 1778	St. Michaels Parish	CC	420-421
Stokes, Grace			S	37-38
Stokes, Joseph	4 Mar 1763		V	368
Stoll, David	27 Nov 1771		Z	189-192
Stoll, Jacob	29 Sep 1768		X	394
Stoll, Mary	14 Jul 1772	Charlestown	&	138
Stone, Benjamin Senr	17 Jan 1758		T	64-67
Stone, Miss Jane	1 Nov 1771		Z	136
Stone, John	4 May 1761	Charles Town	V	8-9
Stone, Joseph	10 Dec 1757	St. Thomas Parish	S	269-271
Stone, Martha	14 Aug 1759		T	237-238
Stone, Revd Robert	3 Dec 1751		R(1)	139-140
Stone, Thomas	4 Jan 1768	Beaufort	X	249
Storey, Elliott	1 Jul 1755	Beaufort[?]	R(2)	364
Storey, John	8 Sep 1767		Y	11-13
Stott, Robt. & Nathaniel	29 Sep 1772		Z	270-288
Stoutenburg, Luke	17 Feb 1773		&	280-282
Strachan, Capt. John	26 Mar 1757		S	48
Strain, David	1 May 1772		&	112-113
Strain, Margaret	18 Nov 1774	Prince Frederick Parish, Craven Co.	&	492
Streator, James Senr.		St. James Goosecreek Parish	X	376-377
Stringer, Joseph	18 June 1761		T	633-634
Stringham, Hannah	17 Nov 1774		&	469-470
Strobar, Jacob	28 Nov 1767		X	283-284
Stroman, Jacob	14 Mar 1781		BB	150-151
Strother, Benja.			&	15
Strother, Benjamin	6 Dec 1771	Berkley Co.	AA	8
Strother, Charles	11 Jan 1774		Z	469-471
Strother, George	12 Dec 1772		&	253-254
Strother, William	23 May 1751	Congarees	R(1)	40-42
Stuart, Francis	5 Aug 1767	Beaufort	X	101-114
Stuart, James	27 Dec 1758		T	94-95
Stuart, James	11 Jan 1774		Z	471-472
Stuart, Mary	2 Mar 1774		Z	539
Stuart, Patrick	23 Mar 1774	St. Davids Parish	&	337
Sulivan, Josiah	28 May 1758		T	25-26
Sullivan, John	29 Feb 1750/1		B	395
[Sullivan, John]	29 Jan 1777		AA	210
Sumervell, Thomas	1 Jul 1775	St. Marks Parish	AA	221-223
Summer, John	14 Dec 1747		MM	241-242
Summers, James	17 Aug 1754	George Town	R(2)	246-250
Summers, Sarah			T	441
Sumne, Daniel	9 Apr 1753		R(1)	546

Name	Date	Location	Vol. & pages	
Sumner, David			B	10
Sumner, Mary	22 May 1750		B	265
Sumner, Sarah	20 Mar 1748/9	Berkley Co.	B	106-107
Sumner, Samuel	21 Aug 1754		R(2)	168
Sutton, Robert			S	434-435
Swadler, Abraham			T	362-364
Swadler, George	17 Mar 1774		Z	508-510
Swainston, Robert			BB	22-23
Swallow, Newman	13 Apr 1773	Charles Town	Z	326-332
Swan, Robert	23 Aug 1774		AA	3-5; 20
Swann, Edward	13 Apr 1755		R(2)	330-331
Swancy, James	27 Jun 1767	Prince Williams Parish	Y	4
Sweringham, James	21 Sep 1775		BB	73-74
Swindershine, Nicholas	30 May 1774		&	427-428
Swindle, Joshua			Y	147-149
Swink, John Henrick	13 May 1762		V	247
Swint, Doctor John	8 May [1781?]		BB	185-186
Swinton, Alexander	17 Apr 1773		&	231-232
Switzer, Leonard	26 Nov 1767		X	245
Swyers, Israel	5 Oct 1761		V	56
Sym, Elizabeth	19 Aug 1747	Chas. Town	MM	192-193
Syms, Isaac	1 Feb 1747/8		MM	269-272
Talbert, James	6 Jul 1763		V	468-469
Tallman, John Richard	19 Jan 1781		BB	159
Tankard, John	Apr 1749		B	172
Tankard, John	12 Jun. 1769	St. Andrews Parish	X	466-467
Tankard, Sarah	5 Jul 1769		X	469
Tanner, Robt.			&	444-445
Tart, Nathan	24 May 1768		X	328-329
Taylor, Barnard		St. Thoma Parish	R(2)	377-378
Taylor, Catharine widow	21 Apr 1757		S	149
Taylor, Chas.	8 Aug 1774	Chas. Town	&	501
Taylor, James	23 Aug 1776		BB	11
Taylor, James	25 Oct 1758		T	94
Taylor, John			T	112
Taylor, John	5 Jun 1767		X	114-115
Taylor, John	27 Feb 1771		Y	405
Taylor, John	3 Oct 1773		Z	402
Taylor, Jos	5 Apr 1757		S	115-117
Taylor, Peter		Goose Creek	X	191-194
Taylor, Samuel	27 Feb 1768		X	413
Tennis, James			MM	206
Terrell, John	12 Apr 1774	St. Marks Parish, Camden District	&	511-512
Terrey, Stephen	24 Oct 1771		Z	126
Terry, John	2 Mar 1748/9	Charles Town	B	79
Testard, Mary			X	143
Theus, Simeon	12 Nov 1760		T	415-416
Thirk[?], Francis			B	405-407
Thomas, Alexander	23 Apr 1768	Prince Fredericks Parish	X	322
Thomas, Athanasuis	29 Sep 1758		T	50-51
Thomas, Cecilia	2 May 1769	Congarees	X	456
Thomas, Dempson	4 Jul 1770	All Saints Parish, Craven Co.	Y	303-304
Thomas, Elizabeth	6 Oct 1770		Y	330-332
Thomas, John	7 Feb 1756		R(2)	408
Thomas, Rev. John	24 Jan 1772	Charles Town	Z	192-196
Thomas John Jr.	22 Dec 1768		X	406-407
Thomas, Jonathan	14 Jul 1769		Y	102-103
Thomas, Mary Anne	28 Jun 1762	Craven Co.	V	241
Thomas, Mrs. Rebecca	2 Oct 1762		V	284-286
Thomas, Samuel	30 Jul 1764	Ninty Six	W	171-172
Thomas, Samuel			Z	463-469
Thomas, Saml	29 Jan 1773		&	201-203
Thomlinson, John	27 Aug 1776	St. Phillips Parish, Charles Town	&	605
Thomlinson, John	27 Aug 1776	St. Phillips Parish, Charlestown	CC	25

Name	Date	Location	Vol. & pages	
Thompson, Archd.			X	49
Thompson, Francis	14 Apr 1747	Charles Town	MM	82-83
Thompson, Isaac	8 Jun 1768	Craven Co.	X	349
Thompson, Matthew	29 Jul 1777		AA	264
Thompson, Moses	17 Dec 1770		Y	446
Thompson, Coll. Moses	6 Apr 1772		&	35
Thompson, Robert	15 Mar 1775	St. Davids Parish	CC	40
Thompson, Sarah			BB	174
Thompson, William	9 Sep 1773		Z	395
Thompson, Wm	6 Dec 1777	Orangeburgh Dist.	CC	394-395
Thomson, David	31 Dec 1770	Charles Town	Y	420
Thomson, Enoch	24 Oct 1774		AA	53a-54b
Thomson, Hugh	21 Dec 1774	Round O	&	480-483
Thomson, Hugh	21 Aug 1775		&	584-585
Thomson, James	9 Mar 1761		T	488-490
Thomson, John	24 Nov 1763		V	509-511
Thomson, John	27 Dec 1766		W	357-358
Thomson, John	26 Aug 1771	St. Mathews Parish	Z	86
Thomson, John Senior	10 Jan 1758		S	281
Thomson, Michael	30 Mar 1776		CC	1
Thomson, Robert	5 Dec 1763		W	318-319
Thomson, Samuel			S	308-309
Thomson, William	10 Jan 1758		S	280
Thomson, William	22 Apr 1768	Indian Town	X	321
Thomson, Wm.	19 Apr 1774		&	334-335
Thomson, William	7 Feb 1774		&	424-425
Thornton, Robert	29 Oct 1762		V	323
Thornton, Samuel	19 Jun 1770	James Island	Y	313-314
Thorp, Samuel	19 Mar 1778		CC	406-407
Thorpe, Robt	31 Mar 1750	Beaufort, Port Royal	B	254-257
Threadcraft, Sarah	22 Apr 1771		Y	446
Threadcroft, Thomas			B	365
Tidyman, Philip	9 Oct 1780	Santee	BB	134-140
Tighe, Charles	30 Dec 1774	George Town	Z	494-497
Timmerly, Ann	11 May 1774		&	338
Timmons, Richard	17 Dec 1760		T	470-471
Timmons, Thomas	2 Jun 1762		T	629-630
Timmons, Thomas Junr.	19 Apr 1773	St. Bartholomews Parish, Colleton Co.	&	233-234
Timothy, Elizabeth widow	2 Jul 1757	Charlestown	S	164-167
Tison, Samuel	27 Feb 1772		&	22-23
Tison, Samuel	11 Mar 1772	St. Peters Parish	&	447
Tissot, Revd. James	30 Aug 1763		V	521-522
Tobias, Jacob	30 Apr 1777	Charles Town	BB	34
Tobias, Joseph	10 Apr 1761		T	645-647
Tobias, Margaret	21 Aug 1773		Z	403
Tobias, Joseph	4 Jul 1761		V	1
Tobias, Sarah widow	20 Nov 1775	Prince Williams Parish, Beaufort District	&	601
Tobler, John Senr	14 May 1765		W	265-267
Tobler, Ulrick	30 Sep 1762	Granville Co.	V	281-283
Tod, William		Charlestown	BB	104-105
Todd, Robert	10 Apr 1758		S	399-400
Todhanter, Joseph	13 Nov 1765	Charles Town	X	185-189
Tomlinson, Arthur	31 Oct 1767		X	229-230
Tomlinson, Josiah	5 Jun 1761		V	1-4
Tonge, Rev. John	14 Dec 1773	Chas. Town	Z	479-482
Toomer, Caleb	27 Apr 1769		X	452-454
Toomer, Caleb	27 Feb 1773	St. Helena Island	&	212-213
Toomer, David	21 Feb 1775	Prince Williams Parish	&	539-540
Toomer, John	12 Feb 1762		V	153-154
Toomer, Ralph	5 Sep 1766		X	58
Torquet, Paul	30 Mar 1748		MM	292
Torrans, John	14 Dec 1780	CharlesTown	BB	93-95
Toussiger, Stephen	19 Feb 1761		T	281-282
Townsend, Abigail	10 Dec 1773	Wadmellaw Island	Z	487-490
Townsend, Daniel	30 Jan 1746/7	Charles Town	MM	57-66
Townsend, Solomon	3 Nov 1758		T	92-93

Name	Date	Location	Vol.	& pages
Townsend, Tharmozon			&	168
Townsend, Wm.	18 Jan 1768		X	257-258
Trammell, Daniel	31 Dec 1777		CC	402-403
Trapier, Alexander	5 Dec 1772		&	178-179
Trappier, Paul	23 Jun 1758		S	442-444
Travers, Francis			CC	358
Trissell, Nathaniel	12 Feb 1754		R(2)	134
Truchet, Anthony	3 Apr 1762		V	147
Truchet, Marc	4 May 1769		Y	45
Trusler, Edward	6 Aug 1761		V	30-31
Trusler, William	10 Sep 1781		BB	222-224
Tucker, Arthur	15 Jun 1768	St. Bartholomews Parish, Colleton Co.	X	352
Tucker, Arthur			Y	45
Tucker, Edward	17 Feb 1769		Y	36-38
Tucker, Nathaniel	7 Jan 1757	Charles Town	S	12-14
Tucker, Doctor Wm	16 Feb 1782		BB	251
Turk, John	26 & 27 Feb 1756		R(2)	443
Turk, William	13 Nov 1773	Ninety Six District	&	471-472
Turnbul, Walter			X	260
Turnbull, James	24 Nov 1767		Y	34-35
Turner, Jacob	10 Apr 1754		R(2)	178
Turner, James	22 Aug 1767		Y	4-5
Turner, John	22 Apr 1755		R(2)	327
Turner, John	27 Feb 1777		BB	31-32
Turner, Widow	1776	Charles Town	BB	20-21
Turner, Wm	23 Dec 1776	Ninety Six District	CC	123-124
Turner, Thomas	24 Oct 1768		X	403
Tybout, Margaret	25 Jul 1769	Charles Town	Y	111
Tycer, William	28 Jul 1768		X	388
Tycer, Wm	4 Nov 1771	Prince Fredericks Parish	Z	145
Ulrick, John	17 Jun 1772		&	103
Uncles, John	4 Feb 1746/7		MM	80-81
Urquhart, Alexander	18 May 1759		T	188
Urquhart, Leonard	2 Apr 1759		T	171
Vallet, John	2 Nov 1768		X	394
Valley, Thos			X	208
Vanall, Mathew	9 Feb 1757		S	33
Vance, Moses			BB	22
Vanderdussen, Col. Alexander	7 Jun 1758		S	446-450
Vanderdussen, Col. Alexr.	4 Apr 1758		T	1-3
Vanderhorst, Arnolous	23 May 1765		W	255-256
Vanderhorst, Joseph	22 Feb 1749/50		B	251
Vanderhorst, Joseph			X	88-89
Vanderhorst, Capt. William	24 Jul 1767	Christ Church Parish	X	98-99
Vanderwick, Mary	1 Oct 1752		R(1)	472-473
Vanvelsen, Edward	3 May 1748		MM	314-317
Vanvelsin, Garret	9 Feb 1749/50		B	331-332
Vanvelson, William	1 Mar 1762		V	111
Vardell, Thomas	13 Dec 1771		Z	169-171
Vardell, Turner	10 Sep 1772	Berkley Co.	&	143
Varner, Samuel	30 Aug 1776		C	27-28
Varnor, Samuel	30 Aug 1776		&	605
Varworth, John	20 Jan 1749/50		B	214-215
Vaughan, [Evan]	1 Jan 1751		R(1)	446-447
Vaughan, John	28 Sep 1745	Charles Town	B	23-25
Veitch, George	15 Oct 1783		AA	265
Veitch, George	4 Nov 1776		CC	90-91
Verdier, Andrew			W	300-302
Viart, Jacob	8 Nov 1763		V	546-547
Videau, Mrs. Ann	22 Dec 1772	St. Thomas Parish	&	192-194
Villepontoux, Peter	28 Jun 1748		MM	333-334
Villepontoux, Peter	26 Oct 1769		Y	137-138

Name	Date	Location	Vol. & pages	
Vinson, George	3 Jun 1755		R(2)	338-339
Vinson, John	29 Jan 1760		T	277-278
Vouloux, James	15 Dec 1748	Charles Town	B	42-47
Wachter, George	10 Jan 1775	St. Mathews Parish	&	509-510
Waddingham, Samuel	27 Sep 1776		AA	149-151
Wagenfield, John	9 Feb 1768	Black Mingo	X	266-267
Waight, Abraham	29 Oct 1746		MM	22-25
Waight, Isaac	1 Jun 1754	St. Johns Parish	R(2)	254-257
Waight, Jacob	29 Jan 1765	Johns Island	W	228-230
Waight, John	9 Nov 1776		&	641-642
Wainwright, Richard	17 Jun 1758		T	20-21
Waite, Ezra	29 Nov 1769	Charles Town	Y	180-182
Waits, Francis	29 May 1754		R(2)	259-260
Waldburger, Jacob	20 Apr 1770		Y	301-303
Waldron, Isaac	29 Oct 1772	Chas. Tonw	Z	263
Waldron, Jacob	30 Oct 1777		CC	371-373
Walker, George		Charles Town	W	89-90
Walker, James	12 May 1755		R(2)	333-334
Walker, Jehu	25 May 1773		&	254-255
Walker, John	24 Apr 1759		T	184-185
Walker, Richard	7 Apr 1774		Z	549-555
Walker, Samuel	19 Jun 1757		S	155-157
Walker, William	9 May 1772		Z	211-212
Wall, John	5 Jun 1758		T	108
Wall, Margaret	17 May 1764		W	101
Wall, Margarett	17 May 1764		V	359
Wall, Richard	30 Jan 1772		Z	205-206
Wallace, James			R(2)	415
Wallace, Samuel			BB	59-60
Wallace, William	22 Nov 1762		V	462-464
Wallace, William	22 Jan 1774	Charlestown	Z	454
Waller, George	3 Nov 1763	Prince Georges Parish	V	511-513
Wallexelson, Thomas	6 Jul 1752	Congrees	R(1)	420
Walley, Thos			Y	100-101
Walter, William	23 Mar 1767		W	403-406
Walter, William			Y	183-185
Walters, Francis	4 Sep 1765		Y	27
Ward, John	22 Mar 1758	St. Johns	T	134-135
Ward, Joseph	14 Jan 1758		S	301-306
Warden, William	26 Mar 1747		MM	78-80
Waring, Archar	20 Aug 1773		Z	394-395
Waring, Benjamin	24 Mar 1763		V	386-390
Waring, Joseph	5 Feb 1754	St. George's Parish	R(2)	142
Waring, Joseph	5 Dec 1761		V	81-84
Waring, Josiah			R(1)	395-396
Waring, Mrs. Mary	30 Jun 1764	Dorchester	V	280-281
Waring, Richard	25 Apr 1753		R(2)	5-8
Waring, Richard	24 Sep 1756	St. Georges Parish	S	10-12
Waring, Robert			CC	409-411
Waring, Mrs. Sarah	3 May 1756		R(2)	450
Waring, Mrs. Sarah	23 Nov 1757		S	253
Waring, Thomas	31 Jan 1754	St. George's Parish	R(2)	140-141
Waring, Thomas	6 Mar 1758		S	347-349
Warley, Melchior	15 Jun 1781	Charles Town	BB	181-182
Warner, John	24 Apr 1776		CC	22-23
Warnock, Andrew	5 Apr 1750		B	271-272
Warnock, Samuel	19 Dec 1755		R(2)	438
Warring, Sarah	10 Dec 1767		X	219
Warring, Thomas	14 Nov 1765		W	289
Warshing, Abraham	25 Jan 1768		X	253-254
Wascot, John Senior	30 Jun 1764		W	125-126
Waters, Francis	24 Aug 1765	Peedee	X	43
Waterson, John	3 Jan 1775	Ninety Six District	AA	74-76
Waties, John			T	opp. 1
Waties, John	29 Oct 1760		T	454-459
Waties, Mr. John	16 Aug 1764	George Town	W	174
Waties, Thomas	20 Dec 1762		V	326-330

Name	Date	Location	Vol. & pages	
Waties, William			B	427-429
Watkins, William			MM	216-217
Watson, Alexander	10 Feb 1761		T	487-488
Watson, Gilbert	27 Dec [1777]		CC	283-284
Watson, James	13 Jun 1771	Granville Co., St. Helena Parish, Euhaw Indian Land	Z	23-24
Watson, John	21 Jan 1767	Craven Co.	X	139
Watson, John Junr	25 Aug 1748	Chas: Town	B	12-19
Watson, Jonathan	9 Oct 1777		CC	237
Watson, Nicholas	5 Dec 1776		BB	8
[Watson], Thomas	-- Oct ----		MM	227
Watson, William	23 Nov 1757		S	225-226
Watson, William	31 Dec 1759		T	276-277
Watson, William			X	286
Watt, John	10 Dec 1776		CC	91-92
Watts, Ann	14 Dec 1756		S	32
Watts, David	2 Apr 1777		CC	159-160
Waugh, Samuel	1 Dec 1767		X	239
Way, Daniel	2 Apr 1753		R(2)	11
[Way, Henry]			V	286
Way, Nathaniel	21 May 1750		B	265
Way, William	29 Jul 1754		R(2)	135
Wear, James	25 Oct 1769	Black Mingo Creek	Y	236-237
Weatherley, Richard	22 May 1770		Y	239-240
Weatherley, Thos.	1 Jun 1749		B	138-142
Weatherly, Ann	6 Oct 1777		AA	263
Weatherly, Isaac	4 & 5 Dec 1765	St. Helena Island	X	205-208
Weatherly, Richard	3 Nov 1777		CC	265
Weatherly, William	19 May 1761		T	615-616
[Weatherspoon, Philip]	19 --- ----		CC	206-207
Weatherspoon, Mrs. Ruth	25 Oct 1764		W	167
Weaver, George	14 Dec 1767		X	265-266
Weaver, Robert	10 Sep 1772	Mars Bluff, Peedee	&	143-162
Weaver, Thomas			R(2)	258-259
Webb, Mrs. Deborah	27 Mar 1775	Ashepoo	AA	89-90
Webb, Edward	27 Jul 1748		B	12
Webb, John	6 Mar 1756	Charles Town	R(2)	440-441
Webb, John			W	106-107
Webb, Thomas	7 Dec 1769	Berkley Co.	Y	216-217
Webb, Thomas	28 Jul 1772	St. Marks Parish	&	137
Webb, William	13 Apr 1752		R(2)	365-366
Webb, William	8 Mar 1774	St. Bartholomews Parish	Z	518-520
Webster, Henry			Z	196
Weekley, Thomas	17 Jul 1750	Amelia Township, Berkley County	B	298-299
Well, Benjamin	16 Nov 1776	St. Bartholomews Parish	BB	4-7
Wells, Edgar	8 Sep 1756		R(2)	530
Wells, John	10 Aug 1750		R(1)	87-88
Wells, John	25 Jul 1776	St. Pauls Parish	&	612-615
Wells, John	25 Jul 1776	St. Pauls Parish	CC	37-39
Wells, Joseph	24 Jul 1750		B	317-318
Wells, Mary	6 Jun 1751		R(1)	15-16
Wells, Samuel	7 May 1764		W	64-66
Wells, Thomas	28 Jul 1761		V	26-27
Wells, William	12 May 1747		MM	126-127
Welsby, William	20 Jun 1758		T	8-10
Welt, Peter	1777	Charlestown	CC	307-308
Werner, Jacob	21 Jan 1783	Ashley River	BB	264
Werner, John	24 Apr 1776		CC	68
Wernor, Mathew	7 Mar 1767		X	159
Wesbury, Jonathan	16 Dec 1765		X	185
Wesbery, Joshua	20 Jul 1756		R(2)	491
Wesbury, William	27 Jan 1767		W	366
Wescoat, William	5 Nov 1768		X	402
Wescoate, Joseph	26 Apr 1777		BB	9
West, John	25 Mar 1778	Camden District	CC	415
Westbury, Jonathan	22 Feb 1765		W	230
Westbury, Jonathan	30 Mar 1765	St. James, Goose Creek	&	23

Name	Date	Location	Vol. & pages
Westbury, William			B 408
Westbury, William	25 Apr 1752		R(1) 388
Westfield, David			T 67-68
Westfield, John	3 May 1763		V 441-444
Westfield, John	19 Aug 1763		W 2
Weston, Jacob	11 Oct 1768		X 398-399
Weston, William	16 May 1767		X 389
Whaley, Thomas			R(2) 214-215
Whaley, Thomas	6 Mar 1769	St. Bartholomews Parish	X 438-439
Whaley, William	26 Feb 1765		W 250
Wheeler, Rev. Daniel	26 Apr 1777		BB 44
Whildn, Jos.	9 Dec 1777		CC 314-315
White, Coll. Anthony	27 Jun 1747		MM 309-311
White, George	5 May 1767		W 437-438
White, George	20 Apr 1767	Craven Co.	Y 145-146
White, Hannah			& 392-393
White, James	24 May 1774		& 366-367
White, Doctor James	29 Apr 1757		S 150-155
White, John	24 Aug 1757	Prince Wm's Parish	S 177-178
White, Col. John	21 Mar 1761		T 533-535
White, John Plowman			Z 16-17
White, Joseph	24 Nov 1755		R(2) 378
White, Joseph	29 May 1758		S 445-446
White, Joseph	25 May 1772	Prince Georges Parish	& 92-93
White, Joseph Sr.	12 May 1768		X 321-322
White, Robert		St. Marks Parish	X 121
White, Thomas	3 Nov 1762	Moncks Corner	V 292-299
White, Thomas	28 Oct 1779		BB 267-268
White, William	14 Dec 1746	Berkley Co.	S 3
White, William	10 Feb 1777		AA 175
Whitefield, Luke	11 Dec 1767		X 236-237
Whitehead, James	15 Jun 1767		X 76
Whiteside, Thos.	7 Oct 1762		V 286-288
Whitford, Mary			T 130-131
Whitlock, John	18 Jun 1759		T 204-205
Whitter, Jonathn.	22 Jun 1754		R(2) 201-202
Whitlock, John	20 Apr 1759		T 174-175
Wickham, Nathaniel	2 Mar 1746		B 357-360
Wigfall, Benjamin	9 Aug 1777	Chs Town	CC 244-246
Wigfall, Benjamin	1- Aug 1777		CC 342
Wigg, Edward	31 Oct 1755	Port Royal	R(2) 390-393
Wigg, Elenor	24 Nov 1762		V 362
Wigg, Hildersdon	9 Jul 1754	Port Royal	R(2) 336
Wigg, Thomas	28 Apr 1761		T 216-217
Wigg, Thomas Edward	25 Nov 1776		BB 18
Wilberfoss, Wm.	23 May 1753		R(2) 20-30
Wilds, Samuel	16 Nov 1770		Y 344
Wilke, John	30 Sep 1771		Z 127-129
Wilkens, Samuel	28 Mar 1771		Z 46-47
Wilkey, James	10 Jun 1767	Charles Town	W 443-444
Wilkie, John	8 Feb 1754		R(2) 167
Wilkins, Archibald			T 635-637
Wilkins, John	21 Dec 1756		S 2-3
Wilkins, Jonathan			V 245-247
Wilkins, Obadiah	22 Apr 1756		R(2) 489-490
Wilkins, Paul	18 Mar 1768		X 302
Wilkins, William	12 Dec 1764		W 195-196
Wilkins, William	24 Jan 1771	Prince Williams Parish, Granville Co.	Y 392-393
Wilkinson, Christopher	9 Sep 1776		CC 84-90
Wilkinson, Edward Junr	23 Jul 1771		Z 105-113
Wilkinson, Francis	3 Feb 1762		V 91-97
Wilkinson, Joseph	27 Mar 1775		& 560-561
Wilkinson, Mary	11 Feb 1775		& 510
Wilkinson, Robert	12 May 1773	St. Helena Parish	& 268-269
Wilkinson, Robert	24 May 1777		BB 45-46
Willett, Samuel			W 396-397
[William], George	18 Dec 1747		MM 254

Name	Date	Location	Vol. & pages	
Williams, Anthony	24 Mar 1772	St. Marks Parish	&	30
Williams, Daniel	13 Jan 1769	Hilton Head	Y	84-85
Williams, David	1 May 1767	Catfish, Prince George Parish, Craven Co.	W	420-421
Williams, David	10 Sep 1766		W	317-318
Williams, David	14 May 1764	Indian Creek	W	131
Williams, David	14 Dec 1776	St. Davids Parish, Peedee	CC	170-175
Williams, Eleanor	21 Dec 1772	St. Davids Parish	&	190
Williams, James	4 Mar 1772	Beaufort	&	24
Williams, Jehu	4 Apr 1771	St. Davids Parish	Y	453-455
Williams, John	6 Nov 1749		B	179
Williams, John	31 May ----		T	200
Williams, John	21 Jul 1761	St. Stephens Parish	V	32-33
Williams, John	24 Feb 1775		&	509
Williams, John		St. Marks, Santee	BB	16
Williams, Joseph	6 Jul 1769		Y	49-51
Williams, Kezia	18 Feb 1774		Z	490
Williams, Mary	1 Nov 1768		X	394-395
Williams, Michael			Z	147
Williams, Paul	19 Jul 1754		R(2)	232-233
Williams, Philip	26 May 1767		W	444-446
Williams, Robert	21 Oct 1776		CC	133-134
Williams, Rev. Robert	10 Nov 1768	Craven Co.	X	409
Williams, Samuel	1 May 1760		T	326
Williams, Thos.			Y	243
Williams, Thomas	14 Apr 1777		BB	55-57
Williams, William	6 Feb 1761		V	28-29
Williams, William	12 Jul 1770	Charlestown	Z	229-232
Williams, William	26 Jan 1773		&	191
Williams, William	28 Jul 1775		AA	114-116
[Williamson], Benjamin	13 Apr 1748		MM	293-295
Williamson, Benjamin	5 & 7 Mar 1774		Z	542-548
Williamson, Champernown	23 Jan 1769		X	424
Williamson, Elizabeth			T	569-571
Williamson, James		Jacksonburgh	X	133-134
Williamson, John	7 Oct 1766		W	327-328
Williamson, Margaret			B	171-172
Williamson, William	13 Apr 1753		R(2)	3
Williamson, William	9 Dec 1767		X	329-330
Williamson, Wm.	10 Oct 1770	Charles Town	Y	349-350
Williamson, Capt. Wm. Bower	7 Jul 1762		V	234-237
Willply, Dr. Benjamin		near Saltketcher, St. Bartholomews Parish	Z	386-389
Willply, Dr. Benjamin	14 Oct 1777	Charleston	CC	237-238
Wills, Hannah	12 Sep 1777		AA	256
Willson, Willson	12 Oct 1746	George Town	MM	45-47
Wilmhurst, John	13 Jun 1774	Charlestown	&	459
Wilson, David	14 Mar 1758		S	363
Wilson, Esther	14 Mar 1775		&	552-553
Wilson, Hugh	28 Jan 1775		AA	82-84
Wilson, James	3 Apr 1750		B	242-243
Wilson, James	28 Sep 1773	Charles Town	Z	444-445
Wilson, James	18 Sep 1776	Prince Williams Parish	AA	161-162
Wilson, John	28 Jan 1765	Charles Town	W	224-225
Wilson, John	12 May 1766		Y	27-28
Wilson, John	4 Nov 1776	Congarees, Camden Dist.	AA	165-166
Wilson, Margarett			MM	254-255
Wilson, Mary	11 Aug 1756		R(2)	521
Wilson, Mathew	1 Nov 1764	Stono landing	W	188-190
Wilson, Ralph	2 Oct 1776		&	618
Wilson, Thos	5 Feb 1771		Y	417-419
Wilson, Thomas	27 Jun 1774	Ninety Six District	&	395-396
Wilson, Thomas	10 Oct 1776		AA	67-68
Wilson, William	-- Aug 1761		V	37-43
Wilson, William	15 Apr 1763	Black Mingo	V	373-374
Wilson, William	15 Nov 1764	Charles Town	W	182-186

Name	Date	Location	Vol. & pages	
Wilton, Rev. Joseph Dacre	9 Nov 1767		X	213-216
Wiltshire, Thoams	26 Nov 1773	St. Michaels Parish, Charlestown	Z	412-413
Winborn, Samuel	25 May 1762		V	215-221
Winborn, Susanna	1 Jan 1781		BB	121-122
Winborn, Tho.	1762		V	176-177
Winborn, Thomas	3 -- 1756	St. John's Parish	R(2)	483-485
Windburn, Ichabod			MM	202-205
Wineman, Leonard	28 Jan 1764		W	35-36
Wingate, Ann	31 Jan 1774		Z	533-534
Wingate, Edward	15 Jun 1761	Craven Co.	V	11-12
Wingood, John	24 Apr		R(1)	35
Wingood, John	19 Mar 1765		W	228
Wirshing, Jacob	30 Oct 1758		T	68
Wirth, Jacob	28 Jul 1770		Y	328-330
Wirth, Philip	12 Sep 1771		Z	98-99
Wise, David	1 Aug 1772	Charlestown	Z	228
Withers, Francis	15 Aug 1771		Z	92-98
Withers, James			R(2)	538-543
Withers, Mary	8 Oct 1767		X	233-234
Witherspoon, David	19 Dec 1759		T	269
Witherspoon, Elizabeth	23 Apr 1777		BB	40
Witherspoon, Gavin	19 Dec 1774		&	513-514
Witherspoon, James	20 Jan 1769	Williamsburgh, Craven Co.	X	428
Witherspoon, James Jr.	9 Feb 1774		&	324
Witherspoon, Robert	27 Jan 1759		T	159
Witten, Robt.	19 Jul 1774		&	448-449
Witter, Benjamin	23 Nov 1749		B	211-212
Witter, Benjamin	20 Sep 1764	James Island	W	153
Witter, James	13 Oct 1746		MM	43-45
Witter, James Junr.	20 --- 1777		AA	188
Witter, John	13 Oct 1746		MM	42-43
Witter, John	8 Jun 1758		T	33-35
Witter, Samuel	-- Nov 1755		R(2)	379
Witter, Thomas	21 Jul 1749		B	148-150
Wolf, John Lewis	9 Nov 1770	Orangeburgh	Y	343-344
Wolferston, Lawrence	8 May 1756	Beaufort	R(2)	511-521
Wood, Alexr	28 Feb 1757	Goosecreek	S	157-162
Wood, Ann	9 Dec 1780	Chas. Town	BB	160-167
Wood, Benjamin	21 Sep 1752		R(1)	447-450
Wood, Henry Senr.	19 May 1758		S	400-402
Wood, George	6 May 1777		BB	60-64
Wood, John	6 Dec 1768		X	405
Wood, John	16 Dec 1771		Z	143-145
Wood, Jonathan	22 May 1749		B	105-106
Wood, Joseph	18 June [1775]	St. Davids Parish	AA	103-108
Wood, Robert	9 Dec 1746		MM	54-55
Wood, William	10 Aug 1747	Charles Town	MM	172-176
Wood, William	14 Feb 1761		T	472-473
Woodbery, John	5 Dec 1766		W	359
Woodcraft, Mrs. Martha	22 Sep 1768		X	390-391
Woodroft, Richard	25 Oct 1756		R(2)	557
Woods, Archd.	6 Mar 1769	Granville Co.	X	448
Woods, Archibald	13 Dec 1769		Y	162
Woodsides, Mrs. Sarah	1 Dec 1770		Y	366
Woodward, Sarah		Prince William Parish, Granville Co.	B	266-267
Woolford, Elizabeth	31 Jan 1769		X	440-441
Wornock, John	10 May 1754		R(2)	182
Wornock, Mary	9 Jan 1758	Berkley Co.	S	286-288
Worrel, William	6 Mar 1777		CC	334-335
Wragg, John	5 Aug 1780		BB	84
Wragg, Joseph	18 Sep 1751		R(1)	72-81
Wragg, Joseph	24 Feb 1752	Saltketcher	R(2)	38-40
Wragg, William	7 Jan 1779	Charles Town	BB	87-92
Wrand, Wm	2 Feb 1781	Christ Church Parish	BB	120-121
Wright, Anthony	10 Apr 1762		V	185-186

Name	Date	Location	Vol. & pages	
Wright, Daniel	-- Jun 1755		R(2)	352-353
Wright, George	17 Jan 1775		CC	63-64
Wright, Miss Gibbon			T	403-404
Wright, James	19 Dec 1746		MM	75-78
Wright, James	1 Nov 1762		V	314-317
Wright, James	23 Jul 1777		AA	250-251
Wright, Mary	28 Jan 1761		T	504-505
Wright, Mrs. Mary	26 Mar 1761		T	529
Wright, Richard	13 May 1745	Charles Town	MM	112-121
Wright, Robert	14 Dec 1772		&	185
Wright, Thomas	13 Aug 1766		W	304-305
Wright, Thomas			W	423
Wright, Thomas	14 May 1776	Prince Georges Parish	CC	11-12
Wright, William		Prince Fredericks Parish	R(2)	296
Wurtzer, Henry	7 Mar 1760		T	283-284
Wyatt, Mrs. Mary	24 Jul 1769		Y	113
Wyly, Samuel	20 Jul 1768		X	373
Yales, Robert	20 Nov 1771		&	10-11
Yancey, Charles			CC	412
Yates, Elisha	4 May 1776		CC	6
Yates, James	24 Oct 1774		AA	39-40
Yates, Thos.	5 Apr 1780	Ninety Six District	BB	269
Yeats, James		St. Helenas Parish	Y	322-323
Yenworth, Mary	16 Aug 1756		R(2)	506-508
Yonge, Mrs. Elizabeth	16 Dec 1758		T	97-98
Yonge, Francis Senr	10 Jan 1781	St. Pauls Parish	BB	101-103
Yonge, Robert			R(1)	334-338
You, Charles	7 Aug 1771		Z	57-58
You, Danl	24 Jan 1749/50		B	221
You, John	7 Feb 1749/50		B	220
Young, Alexander	28 Mar 1763		V	438
Young, Archd.	24 Jul 1749	Charles Town	B	162-163
Young, Bernard			T	438
Young, Edward	22 Mar 1765	St. Mark's Parish	W	260-261
Young, Elizaebth			W	186
Young, Francis	17 & 18 Jun 1755	Craven Co.	R(2)	356
Young, Isom	4 Dec 1756		S	21-22
Young, John	30 Mar 1768		X	270-271
Young, Obedience			T	338-340
Young, William	2 Apr 1772		&	29
Young, William	22 Apr 1772	St. Georges Parish	&	63-68
Youngblood, Henry	16 Jul 1770	Colleton	Y	304-306
Youngblood, William	16 Jun 1770		Y	284-285
Yutsey, Valentine	27 Jan 1772		Z	174-176
Zubly, David	Purisbourg	22 Mar 1757	S	117-118

www.ingramcontent.com/pod-product-compliance
Lightning Source LLC
Chambersburg PA
CBHW031428290426
44110CB00011B/572